Guided Reading Management
Structure and Organization
for the Classroom
(Grades 1-3)

Books by Patricia Pavelka

Making the Connection:
Learning Skills Through Literature (K-2)

Making the Connection:
Learning Skills Through Literature (3-6)

Create Independent Learners:
Teacher-Tested Strategies for ALL Ability Levels

Guided Reading Management
Structure and Organization
for the Classroom (1-3)

by
Patricia Pavelka

Edited by
Lois Schenking

Illustrated by
Deborah
Gillette-Youngblood

Husky Trail Press LLC

East Lyme, CT

Copyright © 2002, Patricia Pavelka

Husky Trail Press LLC
PO Box 705
East Lyme, CT 06333
860-739-7644
888-775-5211
860-691-8066 fax
www.huskytrailpress.com

Editor: Lois Schenking
Cover and book illustrations: Deborah Gillette-Youngblood

ISBN No. 0-9722918-0-6

Dedication

To Pat Terry and Pam Terry, who have demonstrated that anything is possible as long as we have faith, family, and friends. Thank you for your endless support and love.

Acknowledgements

To Mom, my role model for life.

To Lois Schenking, a talented educator and straight-forward editor, who was my teacher.

To Ken, my "Mac Man" and special friend.

To Katherine Cloonan, whose guidance and friendship is truly valued.

To Lorraine Walker, publisher of my first three books, whose suggestions and ideas have made this a better resource and book.

To all the teachers who educate our children and who have shared their students' creations with me, including:
> Pacifica Casserta,
> Megan Ragozzine,
> Kelley Auringer,
> Heather Dulka.

And to Richard LaPorta, more than a publisher, he is my inspiration and brother.

Table of Contents

Introduction

Part 1
Organizing and Scheduling Guided Reading Groups

Part 2
What Are the Other Students Doing While I Am With a Guided Reading Group?

Part 3
Organizing and Scheduling Center Work and Assignments

Getting Started Step By Step

Guided Reading Groups

Coordinating Center/Work Groups with Guided Reading Groups

Coordinating Center/Work Groups, Guided Reading Groups, and Background Groups

Quick Overview of Activities

Part 4
Appendix

Appendix Index

Introduction

As I travel our country working with educators, the same message and concern is being voiced: It is not the guided reading instruction that teachers are having difficulty with, it's the management piece.

> How many groups a day can I realistically take?
> How do I structure my classroom?
> What are the other kids doing?
> My students cannot work independently.
> I'm always interrupted while working with guided
> reading groups.

There are many resources available for teachers in the area of guided reading instruction. (There is an extensive bibliography of these resources at the end of this book.) However, there are limited resources available for teachers to get help with the management piece.

The purpose of this book is to help teachers with the structure and management of their classrooms during guided reading instruction. This is not a theory book, nor is it a book about guided reading instruction. Guided Reading Management: Structure and Organization for the Classroom will show you specific easy-to-implement structures, strategies, ideas, and activities to put all of the components of managing Guided Reading together successfully. This book is an "I can do it tomorrow" kind of resource. Suggestions read about today can be implemented in classrooms tomorrow.

This book is divided into four parts:

Part 1: Organizing and Scheduling the Groups

This part shows very specific ways to organize and schedule 4 or 5 guided reading groups. There are a variety of different schedules from which to choose depending upon your specific classroom needs. This section also describes two activities that a group of students may be doing as they work next to the guided reading group. Book Boxes and Literature Discussion Boxes are described in detail.

Part 2: What are the other students doing while the teacher is with a guided reading group?

This part gives a wealth of assignments and activities that students can be working with while the teacher is instructing a guided reading group. These assignments are multi-leveled so that struggling learners as well as proficient learners will benefit from them. The assignments are organized into six different categories:

      Writing
      Listening
      Literature Connections
      Phonics, Spelling and Related Skills
      Sight Vocabulary
      Additional Activities

These assignments are presented in a way that shows how they can be utilized as learning centers or as independent seatwork. The suggested assignments can also be coordinated with your curriculum and books.

Part 3: Organizing and Scheduling Center Work and Assignments

This part shows how to get started step-by-step. There is a schedule for the first four to five weeks of implementing the ideas, activities and strategies in this book. There are examples of rotation charts that help manage your centers and assignments.

Part 4: Appendix

This part provides reproducibles of activities and strategies discussed. These may be copied and used immediately in classrooms. Also provided is an extensive bibliography of educational resources: professional books, children's books and other materials.

Part 1

Organizing and Scheduling Guided Reading Groups

Organizing and Scheduling
Five Guided Reading Groups

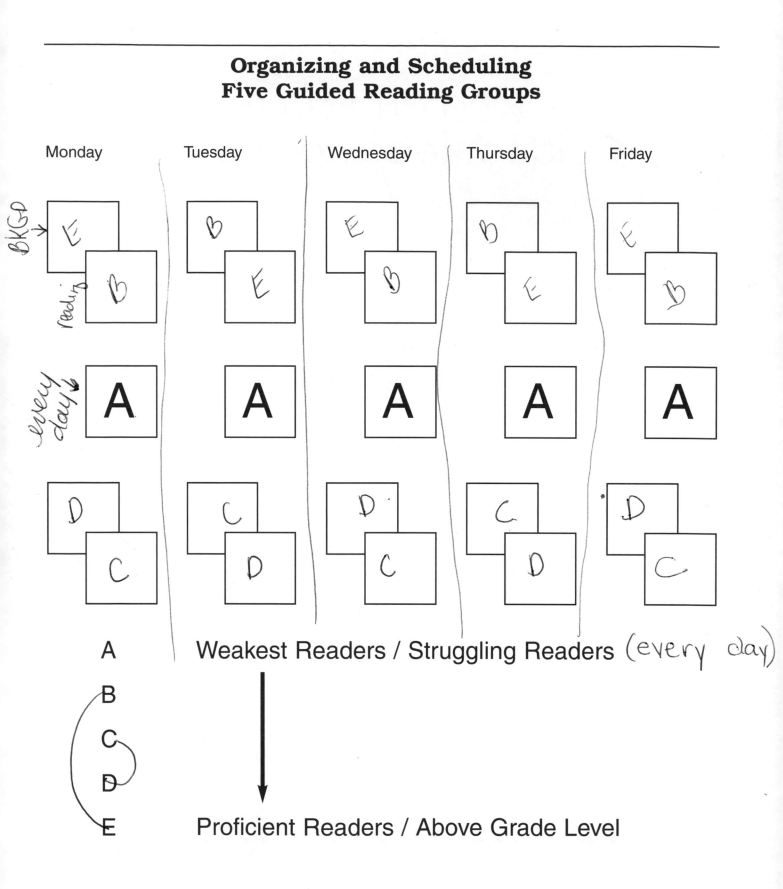

Monday	Tuesday	Wednesday	Thursday	Friday

A   Weakest Readers / Struggling Readers (every day)

↓

E   Proficient Readers / Above Grade Level

Organizing and Scheduling Five Groups

One of the most difficult tasks when implementing guided reading is the management piece. How many groups a day will I take? What will my schedule look like? Do I take all groups every day? This section will address these questions and more.

If you are working with four groups of students turn to page 23.

To the left is a schedule for working with five groups. Each of the five guided reading groups is represented by squares. Groups should be limited to no more than six students.

The guided reading groups are leveled so that you have groups of students who are working at their instructional levels. The five groups will show a range of reading abilities. You will use the following scale:

Group A is the neediest group of students. These are your most fragile readers who need a lot of support and instruction. These are students who may have reading difficulties. These are students the teacher is concerned about.

Group E is your most proficient group of readers. These are students who are either learning the reading process very quickly and easily or are fluent readers.

Groups B, C, and D are in corresponding order of their instructional levels. B is the second "neediest" group while D is the second "highest" group. C is the median group.

You want to take group A every day. These are students who need as much support in their reading development as possible. In the diagram to the left, they are the center group.

You now have four groups left. Pair a less-abled group with a more independent group. You could pair up the four remaining groups the following ways:

Group B and Group D   Group C and Group E

OR

Group B and Group E   Group C and Group D

For example, we will pair groups B & E together and groups C & D together.

Groups B and E are always called to meet at the same time. One group works with the teacher in a guided reading group while the other group is the background group. The front square represents the group that will be working with the teacher in guided reading. The back square represents the background group. The background group will meet to the left or right of the guided reading group and work with reading boxes or literature discussion boxes. (These boxes and the organization of the background groups are explained in detail starting on page 26.)

Each day groups B and E reverse places. See the diagram below.

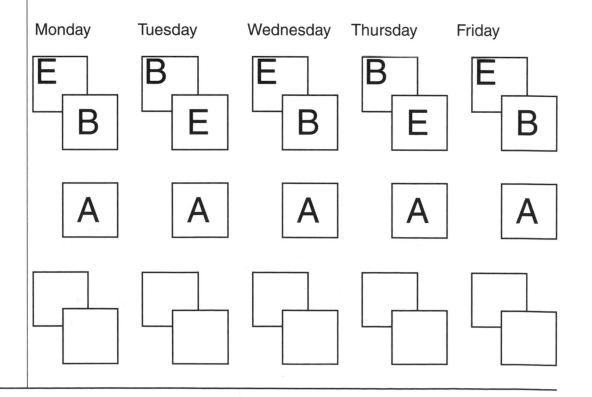

| Monday | Tuesday | Wednesday | Thursday | Friday |

Groups C and D are always called to meet at the same time. One group works with the teacher in a guided reading group while the other group is the background group. The front square represents the group that will be working with the teacher in guided reading. The back square represents the background group. The background group will meet to the left or right of the guided reading group and work with reading boxes or literature discussion boxes.

Each day groups C and D reverse places. See the diagram below.

assess 2 children from bkgd group/day

Monday	Tuesday	Wednesday	Thursday	Friday
E / B	B / E	E / B	B / E	E / B
A	A	A	A	A
D / C	C / D	D / C	C / D	D / C

On Monday, Wednesday, and Friday the teacher meets with groups B, A, and then C for 20 minute guided reading lessons each. Groups E and D work as background groups.

On Tuesday and Thursday, the teacher meets with groups E, A, and then D for 20 minute guided reading lessons each. Groups B and C work as background groups.

You work with your neediest readers five days a week (A), your developing readers three days a week (B&C), and your independent readers two days a week (D&E).

This scheduling format is very flexible depending upon the needs of your students. On the following pages are some options from which to choose. Each option is a two-week cycle.

Option 1 Start with a different group of the paired groups each Monday.

Weekly Schedule 1 (Weeks 1, 3, 5, 7, 9, etc.)

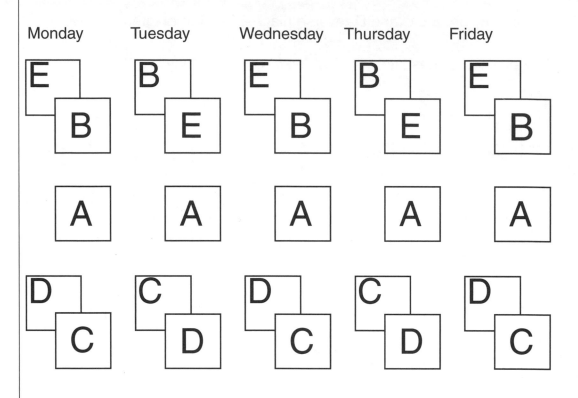

| Monday | Tuesday | Wednesday | Thursday | Friday |

This week groups B & C meet with the teacher three times. Groups D & E meet with the teacher two times. Group A meets with the teacher every day.

Option 1 (continued)

Weekly Schedule 2 (Weeks 2, 4, 6, 8, 10, etc.)

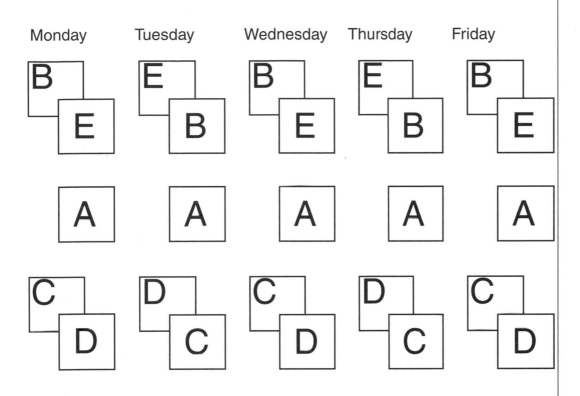

This week groups D & E meet with the teacher three times. Groups B & C meet with the teacher two times. Group A meets with the teacher every day.

Option 2 If there are two groups of students that you are concerned about (groups A and B), then have them reverse places each week.

Weekly Schedule 1 (Weeks 1, 3, 5, 7, 9, etc.)

This week Group A works with the teacher in a guided reading format five days. Group B works with the teacher in a guided reading format three days.

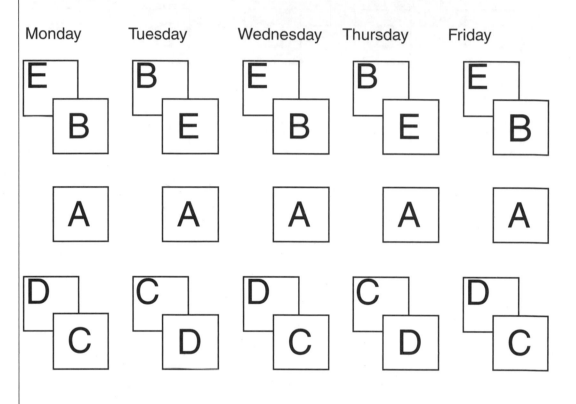

| Monday | Tuesday | Wednesday | Thursday | Friday |

This week Group C works with the teacher three times. Groups D & E work with the teacher two times.

Option 2 (continued)

Weekly Schedule 2 (Weeks 2, 4, 6, 8, 10, etc.)

This week Group B works with the teacher in a guided reading format five days. Group A works with the teacher in a guided reading format three days.

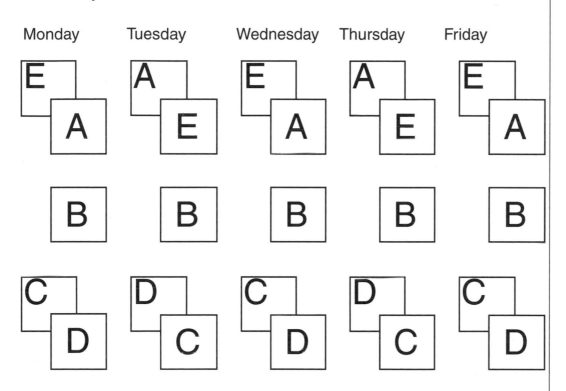

| Monday | Tuesday | Wednesday | Thursday | Friday |

This week Group D works with the teacher three times. Groups C & E work with the teacher two times.

In the Appendix is a blank reproducible of these scheduling boxes. I used a two week cycle for my guided reading groups. The first two pages of my planbook were these scheduling sheets. I always knew which groups I was taking without having to search and rewrite the schedule each week.

Organizing and Scheduling
Four Guided Reading Groups

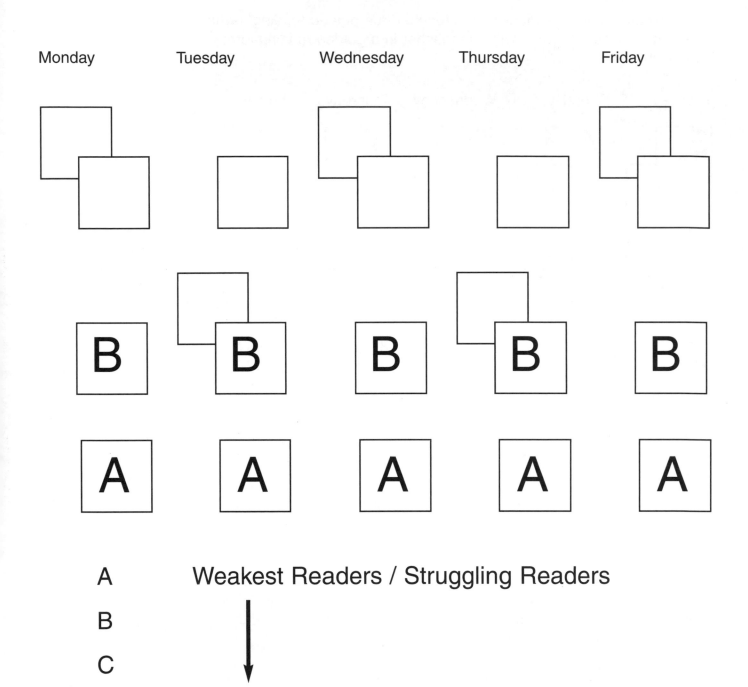

| Monday | Tuesday | Wednesday | Thursday | Friday |

A   Weakest Readers / Struggling Readers

B

C

D   Proficient Readers / Above Grade Level

Organizing and Scheduling
Four Groups

To the left is a schedule for working with four groups. Each of the four guided reading groups is represented by a square.

The guided reading groups are leveled so that you have groups of students who are working at their instructional levels. The four groups will show a range of reading abilities. You will use the following scale:

Group A is the neediest group of students. These are your most fragile readers who need a lot of support and instruction. These are students who may have reading difficulties.

Group B is the next neediest group of students. These are students who would also greatly benefit from being taken every day by the teacher.

Group C has students who are approximately at grade level.

Group D is your most proficient group of readers. These are students who are either learning the reading process very quickly and easily or are fluent readers.

You want to take groups A and B every day. These are students who need as much support in their reading development as possible. The diagram to the left shows groups A and B meeting with the teacher daily for guided reading.

You now have two groups left, C and D. Groups C and D are taken every other day for guided reading. While one group works with the teacher in guided reading, the other group is a background group.

The front square is the group that will be working with the teacher in guided reading. The back square represents the background group. The background group will meet to the left or right of the guided reading group and work with reading boxes or literature discussion boxes. (These boxes and the organization of the background groups are explained in detail starting on page 26.) Below is a two-week cycle schedule.

Weekly Schedule 1

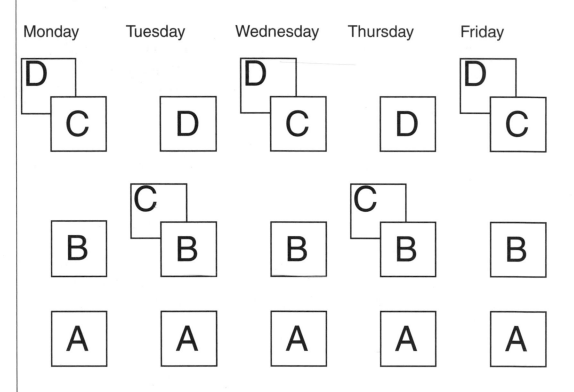

This week groups A and B work with the teacher in a guided reading format all five days. Group C works with the teacher three days and group D works with the teacher two days in a guided reading format.

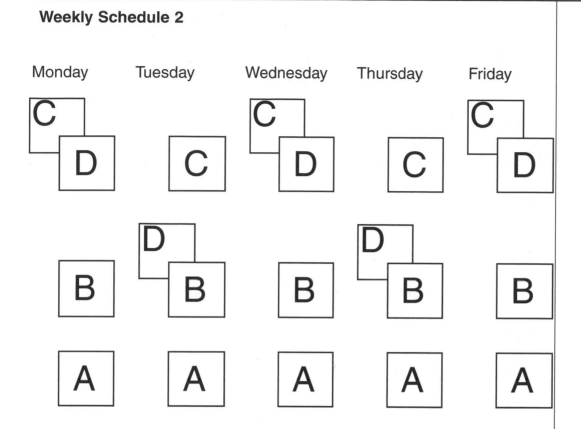

This week groups A and B work with the teacher in a guided reading format all five days. Group D works with the teacher three days and group C works with the teacher two days in a guided reading format.

In the Appendix is a blank reproducible of these scheduling boxes. I used a two-week cycle for my guided reading groups. The first two pages of my planbook were these scheduling sheets. I always knew which groups I was taking without having to search and rewrite the schedule each week.

Background Groups

A background group is a group of students who work together to the left or right of the guided reading group that is meeting with the teacher. This group is, in reality, a guided reading group that is not meeting with the teacher but working independently next to him/her.

Background groups are used for a number of reasons. The first reason is for "crowd control." If your class size is 25 students and you call five students to work with you, there are 20 other students "out there" working alone. If you can get another 5 or 6 out of the "mainstream," it makes a big difference! Instead of five students working with you, there will be 11 students working either with or near you.

The background group is much more "on task" with its assignments because of the close proximity to you. You can give the same assignment to those out there in the "mainstream," but they probably will not be as much on task as when they have been called up by you and working close to you. There are also less distractions when they are working as a background group.

The background groups are working with one of two things:

literature discussion boxes (beginning on page 42)
or
reading boxes (described on the following pages).

Reading Boxes

Reading boxes are used by emergent and beginning readers who need to be reading short, familiar stories and texts over and over again to increase fluency, build sight vocabulary, and increase comprehension.

Reading boxes are also used by fluent readers who are not comfortable with or motivated to read long books/novels.

Quick Overview of Reading Boxes

What are reading boxes?

Reading boxes are boxes or plastic tubs of reading materials created especially for each guided reading group to use when it is meeting as a background group.

How are the reading boxes organized?

The reading materials in the boxes are leveled to be as perfect a match as possible for each group of students. Materials are at students' independent reading levels.

Who uses reading boxes?

The background groups use their designated reading boxes.

When are reading boxes used?

Reading boxes are used by a background group while the teacher is working with a guided reading group.

Where are reading boxes used?

Reading boxes are used on the floor or at a table that is located directly to the right or left of the teacher and his/her guided reading group.

Why are reading boxes created and used?

Students are reading silently at their independent level. They are practicing, utilizing, and applying reading strategies.

Preparation For Reading Boxes

Preparation of the Classroom

Colored Sitting Circles

Make six large different colored circles (one being white) using 9x12 oaktag. Laminate the circles to make them more durable. Tape them on the floor as shown in the diagram below. These circles will help students find their places quickly when they are called to meet as a background group. Students can sit on any color they wish or they may be assigned a color by the teacher.

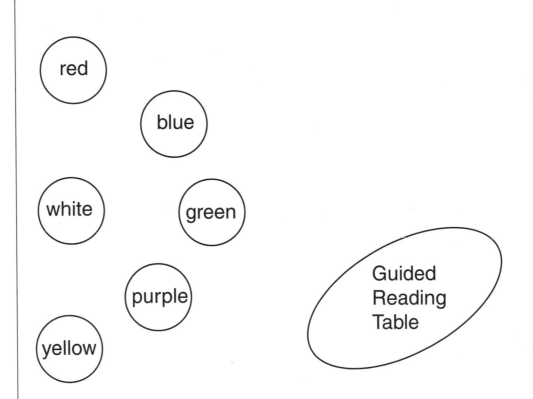

If you have a table available, tape the circles on the backs of the chairs that are around the table. Students can sit on any chair they wish, or they may be assigned a color by the teacher.

Preparation of the Outside
of the Reading Boxes

Front of Reading Boxes

Laminate one blank 5x7 index card
for each reading box. Put a card on
the front of each reading box. Write
the names of students in the group
that will using that particular box for
reading. Because the index card is
laminated, you can add or move
names easily to keep the groups
flexible.

Put a sticker next to the first name on the index card. This student is
the Reader of the Day. Each time the background group meets and
works with its reading box, the sticker gets moved to the next person.
Each child gets a turn to be the Reader of the Day. The Reader of the
Day is explained on pages 35-36.

Back of Reading Boxes

Laminate three blank 5x7 index cards for each reading box. Put the
three cards on the back side of each reading box. These cards will be
used for activities to make the reading boxes manipulative for students
(explained on pages 38-41).

SSR
attend to print
and pictures

Preparation of Materials for the Inside of the Reading Boxes

Colored Circle Cards

Using 5x7 index cards, make a set of cards for each reading box with colored circles that match the colored sitting circles placed on the floor or on chairs (see page 28).

Highlighter Tape Cards

Highlighter tape is tape that is reusable and comes in florescent colors. Students can put it on and take it off pages of books.

You need three pieces of 9x12 white construction paper. Using a magic marker, draw five lines horizontally across each piece of paper to make six equal sections. Laminate the papers.

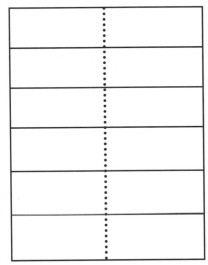

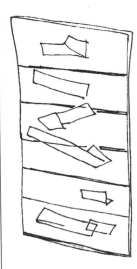

Cut the laminated, lined paper in half vertically so you have six cards measuring 4 1/2" x 6". Take the highlighter tape and cut it into strips. Place the strips of highlighter tape on the six spaces on each card.

Be sure to make a "grab tab" on each strip of tape. Turn one edge of each piece over so that the end is not sticky. This is where students will grab the tape to put it on and take it off when finished. Each student will have his/her own strip of paper with tape.

Inside the Reading Box

When boxes are initially created they are filled with familiar, old favorite reading materials.

> # Familiarity with books allows students to be independent and easily apply, practice, and utilize reading strategies

When first creating reading boxes, I thought the ideal items to put in the boxes would be the small books that students worked with in guided reading groups. However, there are situations where classrooms have a limited number of guided reading books to use. If such books are put into the boxes, it could affect the inventory needed for instruction in the actual guided reading groups. If the goal is to get students reading, then you do not need to limit yourself to using just books.

The following items have been used very successfully in reading boxes.

⭐ Class Lists

Regina

Students are so excited to read each others' names. Make a list of names of students in your class. For young children put pictures of classmates next to their names to help with the reading. Students often pair up and one person reads the first name while the other reads the last name.

School Lists

The class lists were so successful that we created school lists in the reading boxes. School lists are names of any persons that are associated with the school. Your list may include: principal, secretary, teachers, custodians, cooks, crossing guards, bus drivers, etc. Put pictures next to the names for younger children.

Box Books

Box books are great ways to use environmental print. Have students bring in cereal or similar boxes. Cut the top and bottom off the boxes. The boxes will now fold down flat. Put 3-5 boxes together, punch two holes, and tie together with yarn or use chicken rings to put them together into a box book.

There are so many things that can be done with the boxes in addition to using them as books of environmental print. Before you cut and tie the boxes together, use them for graphing activities. For example, have students bring in breakfast food boxes. Graph them according to the ones you eat hot or cold, ones you eat with a fork, spoon or by hand, etc. The same can be done with animal boxes: dog bones, guinea pig food, parrot food, peanuts, cat food, etc. Simple greeting cards can also be used.

Nuts about Reading
Cereal for Learners

Book Covers

Many hard covered books have a book jacket on them. If the actual hard cover of the book has the exact picture as the book jacket, take the cover off. Put three or four book covers together, punch holes and tie them together. These can be used in similar fashion as the box books. Your librarian can be a great resource for this activity.

(handwritten margin notes)
- put a laminated card ie. ch, short a, -at family
- highlight those words on the cereal box
- laminate cereal boxes, give overhead markers, kids can
- trace words
- find (circle) words
- stay away from pictures

Wordless Books

The students' language development increases as they tell stories about the wordless books. Storytelling helps students organize and sequence a story orally. They work with the concepts of beginning, middle, and end, as well as story elements. These books help students attend to pictures.

Books

Two requirements need to be met by books before they can be placed in reading boxes. First, they need to be familiar to the students. Students must have worked with or heard the story at least one time. Second, the books need to be at students' independent reading levels.

Poems

Seasonal poems are fun for students to read over and over again. I found that poetry books were a bit overwhelming for some students. Take the books apart and put in only a couple of poems at a time. You could also type or write the poems out on paper and place the papers in the reading boxes. (See Appendix for recommended poetry books).

Songs and Raps

Coordinate songs with your music teacher. Any song or rap that students are learning is placed in the reading boxes.

Magazines

Weekly Reader, Scholastic News or any other weekly/monthly newsletter that you use in your classroom can be placed in the reading boxes. Sometimes these reading materials are only looked at and discussed one time by the whole class. Utilizing them again for the reading boxes gets some repeated reading of content area materials for students.

→ Write a story about pictures
→ 1st grade label words on pictures find "L words" write them

Pledge of Allegiance

Listen to your students recite the pledge. Many of them really do not know what the words are. Make copies of the Pledge of Allegiance and add them to reading boxes.

Science and Social Studies Connections

Take some important paragraphs from your science and social studies curriculum. Type or write so the print is large for students as expository text can be more difficult for them to read and understand than narrative texts.

Comics

These are short, quick reads for students.

Charts and Chants From Around Your Room

Anything that is displayed in your room can be copied or typed and put in the box. I found that my students often read the things on the wall only when I took them over to them and we did some choral and shared reading. Now they are reading those things many times on their own. I have seen a lot of improvement in my whole class reading of chants and charts because students are practicing them more!

 If you have class rules posted, put copies of them in the reading boxes. Look around your room at all the things you hang up for students to read. Any of those items may be used.

Management of the Background Groups when Using Reading Boxes

When you call the groups, B and C for example, group B (guided reading group) comes to the reading table, while group C (background group) goes to its work place which is either on the floor or at a table to the left or right of you. If students are meeting on the floor, they sit on the colored circles. If students are meeting at a table, they sit on chairs.

Reader of the Day

The Reader of the Day is the student who gets the reading box. So while his/her peers are taking their places, he/she is the only one who touches the box. This has alleviated many disagreements within the group about who is in charge of getting the box.

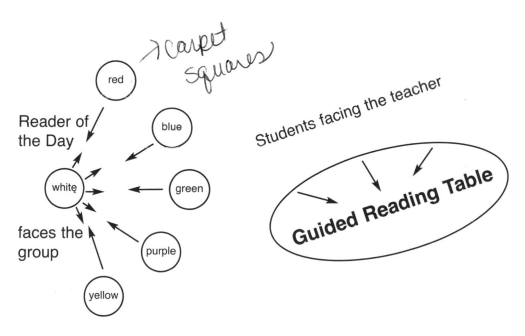

Students in the group face the Reader of the Day

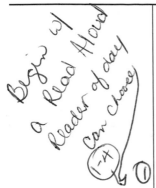
Begin w/
a Read Aloud
Reader of day
can choose
(1-4)

The Reader of the Day begins by choosing a book and reading aloud to the group. This helps the background group start calmly and as a team. It also allows for one child to read orally to an audience.

The Reader of the Day may do any of the following read-aloud activities:

① ## Traditional Read-Aloud

The child reads the material just like the teacher would during a typical read-aloud session. He/she reads and then shows the picture. Any material in the reading box can be done as a traditional read-aloud.

② ## Retelling of the Story

This procedure can be done with only two items: wordless books or books with print. If the Reader of the Day chooses a wordless book, then he/she tells a story as the pictures are shown. The Reader of the Day could also retell any book in the box. The student must tell the group that he/she is retelling the story, not actually reading the book. Often students who are not confident readers choose this method.

③ ## Choral Reading with the Whole Group

The Reader of the Day picks any reading material from the box and the group choral reads it together.

④ ## Popcorn Reading

The Reader of the Day reads a page aloud, and then asks a group member to reread that page aloud. The reading task goes back and forth between the leader and group members.

The Reader of the Day may decide to do this same procedure in the opposite order. He/she shows a page to a group member who will read it aloud, and then the Reader of the Day repeats that page orally.

When the read-aloud is over, students will read silently. The Reader of the Day takes the colored circle cards (see page 30), mixes them up and puts them face-down on the floor. He/she then picks up one card at a time. The child sitting on that chosen color picks his/her reading material first. This routine is continued until all of the students have one item to read.

The Reader of the Day is the last one to choose a reading item from the box. This procedure has stopped the problem of students all pushing and rushing to get into the box first. As students finish reading, they put back their item and choose another on their own. Usually students do not all finish reading at the same time, so each is in the reading box at different times.

There should be about a 3 to 1 ratio of books to students.

Changing Materials in the Reading Boxes

Materials should be changed each month. On the last Thursday or Friday of each month when guided reading groups meet, students work together to clean out and change materials in their reading boxes. First, all of the materials in the reading boxes are taken out. Second, students each put back their favorite reading item. As new books, poems, songs, etc. are worked with during the month they are added to the reading boxes.

Making the Reading Box Manipulative

The following activities are for emergent level readers who may need some hands-on activities to help them focus and attend to the reading materials.

On one side of the box are three laminated index cards. These cards have certain things written on them for students to look for as they read. Using the highlighter tape, students find certain things related to pictures and/or print and mark them. These are optional activities for students to do.

These cards get changed either weekly or every other week.

Index Card #1 - Options

```
characters
```

Write the word "characters" on the index card.

Using picture books with one line of text or less

Students find the characters on each page and mark them with the tape. One of the first prompts used with beginning emergent readers is to look at the pictures. This activity helps students to really attend to and study the pictures.

Using books that have pictures as well as four or more lines of text per page

Students look for illustrations of characters and mark them on each page. Students also mark any text that tells about the character(s). This leads students into making some inferences. For example, the book may not say the character is shy but it can be inferred by the character's actions or how he/she behaves.

```
setting
```

Write the word "setting" on the index card.

Using picture books with one line of text or less

Students look for the setting on each page and mark it with the tape. This again helps students to really attend to and study the pictures.

Using books that have pictures as well as four or more lines of text per page

Students look for the setting on each page and mark it. Students also mark any text that tells about the setting.

highlight the skill

title highlight anything that supports title

title

Write the word "title" on the index card.

Using picture books with one line of text or less

Students look for illustrations that back up and support why the book may have its title. They mark the pictures with the tape. This gives students practice in previewing the title of a book and making predictions about the story.

Using books that have pictures as well as four or more lines of text per page

Students look for illustrations and text that back up and support why the book may have its title. They mark the pictures and text with the tape. This gives students practice in previewing the title of a book and making predictions about the story. It also helps students with comprehension of the story.

red

Put a color word on the index card. Students mark everything in the pictures that is that color.

Index Card #2 - Options

Using the preceding strategy of finding and marking, the following suggestions can be put on the second index card.

Sight words
Letters
Words
Contractions
Verbs with "ing" ending
Verbs with "ed" ending
Plurals
Homophones
Synonyms
Antonyms
Words for "said"

Vowels   punctuation
rhymes

Index Card #3 - Options

Using the preceding strategy of finding and marking, the following suggestions can be put on the third index card.

Anything that corresponds to your phonics and spelling curriculum. For example:

"ay" words
"ai" words
short "a" words
"er" or "ir" words

Assessment of the background group doing these activities is discussed on page 52.

Literature Discussion Boxes

Quick Overview of Literature Discussion Boxes

What are discussion boxes?

Literature discussion boxes are boxes or plastic tubs of reading materials created especially for each guided reading group to use when it is meeting as a background group. These differ from reading boxes because only one title with multiple copies is available as all students will be working with the same book.

How are discussion boxes organized?

The reading material in the box is leveled to be as perfect a match as possible for that group of students. Dictionaries and thesauruses are in the boxes.

Who leads the group's discussions?

Each student will be responsible to lead a specific discussion about something in the book.

When are discussion boxes used?

Discussion boxes are used while the teacher is working with a guided reading group.

Where are discussion boxes used?

Discussion boxes are used on the floor or at a table that is located directly to the right or left of the teacher and his/her guided reading group.

Why are discussion boxes created and used?

Discussion boxes are used with fluent readers to talk about a book in depth. Students come to the group to share and gain insights from each other.

Preparation For Literature Discussion Boxes

Preparation of the Classroom

Chart of Open-Ended Discussion Starters

Make a chart of open-ended discussion starters. These starters need to be applicable to any book. Hang up the chart in your classroom. Below are some suggestions for the chart.

something you liked
your favorite part
something you didn't like
something you want to discuss
a paragraph to read aloud
something about a character
something about the setting
this doesn't make sense
remind you of anything...
know anyone like it...
know any place like it...
ever happen to you...
agree or disagree with the author...
know any other book like this...
know any other character like this...
What is this book really about? (themes)
What would you have done?

to go w/
cube 4, 5, 6

Preparation of Materials for the Literature Discussion Boxes

Front of Literature Discussion Boxes

Laminate one blank 5x7 index card for each reading box. Put a card on one side of each reading box. Write the names of students in the group that will using that particular box for reading. Because the index card is laminated, you can add or move names easily to keep the groups flexible.

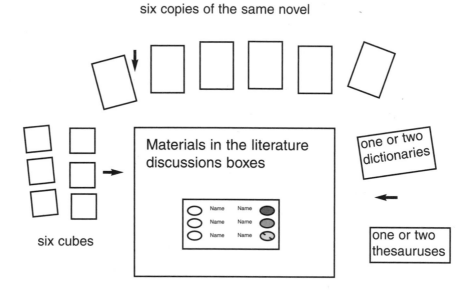

six copies of the same novel

Materials in the literature discussions boxes

one or two dictionaries

six cubes

one or two thesauruses

Each child is assigned a job. Use the index card on the box to designate who has what job. Each child has a dot sticker next to his/her name. Each sticker represents a job (see pages 48-51).

Each week the stickers are moved clockwise to change jobs. Students keep the same job for one week.

Cubes

Using the reproducible found in the Appendix, make three copies of the cube out of oaktag in three different colors.

Cube #1

Label the sides of the first cube with the following:

synonym

antonym

definition

sentence

connect to YOU

importance to the story

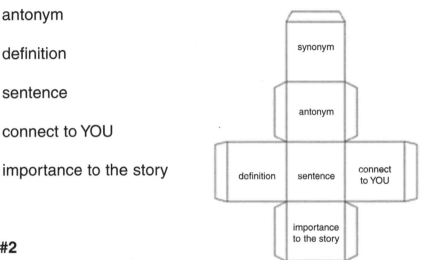

Cube #2

Label the sides of the second cube with the following:

Who

What

Where

Why

When

How

Cube #3

Label the sides of the third cube with the following:

personality: PROVE IT!

physical appearance

your opinion about the character: WHY?

How are you alike?

How are you different?

What has happened to the character in your reading assignmer

Cubes #4, #5, #6

Using the reproducible found in the Appendix, make another three copies of the cube out of oaktag. Coordinate the colors of these three cubes with three colors of the highlighter tape. Write nothing on the sides of these three cubes.

Now that you have your six cubes ready, finish putting them together. Cut out the cubes. Fold on all the lines to form a cube. Stuff the cubes with newspaper or paper towels for added durability. Glue together and then wrap with packaging tape.

Management of the Background Groups when Using Literature Discussion Boxes

Students using discussion boxes are all reading the same book/novel. They come to the group ready to discuss and share perceptions about their reading assignment. You want to create an open-ended dialogue between students in which they extend their learning and move from literal, descriptive talk to a deeper understanding of text.

On the following pages are ideas and suggestions about which jobs students could be doing in the group and how to manage and organize the assignments and discussions. Each job has one cube that helps run the discussion and also helps students manage the group.

When students first arrive at the background group meeting area, they each get their assigned cube from the literature discussion box. They will know what job they are responsible for by looking at the symbol next to their name on the index card on the front of the box.

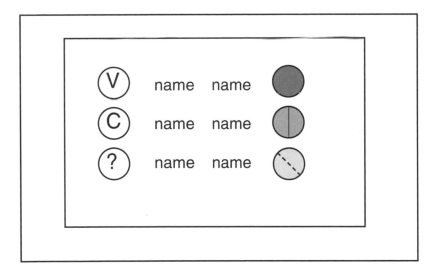

Vocabulary Cube

This job is represented by the sticker that has the letter "V" on it.

Each student brings a vocabulary word from the book to share. This can be a word that was assigned by the teacher or a word chosen by the student. If it is a self-chosen word from the book, students are asked to choose a new, challenging word. Words are written on an index card or piece of paper.

The student in charge of the vocabulary discussion begins first by sharing his/her word with the group. He/she tells what the word is, the definition of the word, and on which page the word is found. All students open their books to that page and find the word. The student in charge reads three sentences: the sentence where the word was found, as well as the sentence before and the sentence after. The student then tells the word's meaning.

After the vocabulary leader has introduced and explained his word, he/she throws the cube to the person on the left. That person rolls the cube and applies the word to whatever side is face-up.

* synonym
> The student gives a synonym for the new vocabulary word. A thesaurus, which is in the box, may be used.

* antonym
> The student tells an antonym for the new vocabulary word.

* definition

> The student gives a definition of the new vocabulary word. The student could either find the word in a dictionary and read the definition or give the meaning in his/her own words.

* sentence

> The new word is used in a sentence by the student. The sentence must be about home, school, or the student. This stops students repeating the sentence from the book.

* connect to YOU

> The student tells how the word is connected to his/her life. For example, if the word was blustery, a connection might be: "I do not like blustery days because I don't like to be cold."

* importance to the story

> The student discusses why that word is important to the story.

After the first person rolls the cube and applies the vocabulary word, it is then thrown back to the leader. The leader then throws it to the next person in a clockwise manner. That student rolls the cube and applies the vocabulary word to what the cube says. This continues until all of the students have rolled the cube and applied cube directions to the newly introduced vocabulary word.

Question Word Cube

This job is represented by the sticker that has a "?" on it.

This job is basically summarizing what was read. The leader begins by telling a summary of the pages read in the story. Students then each take a turn to roll the cube and discuss the question word.

Character Cube

This job is represented by the sticker that has the letter "C" on it.

The leader begins by telling something about the character. He/she then throws the cube to the next person who rolls and shares. Continue until everyone has had a turn to discuss the character.

Rolling the Cube

What if a student rolls the cube and gets the same side that has already been rolled and discussed? Students have three options:

1. Roll the cube again. If the same side comes up again he/she must do either number two or three.

2. A student may repeat the same answer that was just given.

3. A student may give a new answer or restate the given answer in his/her own words.

Color Cubes

This job is represented by the three colored stickers.

Using different colored pieces of highlighter tape, mark three things on the chart of open-ended questions posted in your classroom with the tape. Students will mark the parts of the story that back up and correspond to what was highlighted on the chart. Their tape should match the color of each tape on the chart.

For example, if you take yellow highlighter tape and mark "a paragraph to read aloud," then students will use a piece of yellow tape to mark a paragraph in their books that they wish to read aloud. If you mark "something about the character" in blue, then students will use blue tape and mark something in their books that has to do with the character.

The color cube leader will go first, find his/her marked text, and discuss it with the group. If any students want to respond, they raise their hands and the leader will throw the cube to one of them.

When the leader is done with his/her turn, the cube is thrown to the next person who finds his/her marked text, and discusses it with the group. This continues until all students have shared.

The cubes help to manage taking turns, making sure that everyone gets a turn to share and is an attentive audience participant. The rule is:

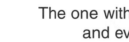

The one with the cube does the talking
and everyone else listens.

The cubes also direct the conversation so that students have a springboard that leads to critical and thought-provoking discussions.

Assessment of Background Groups

When your guided reading instruction is complete, give them a three to four minute activity to do independently. If they are tired and unable to focus anymore, give them some clay to make letters, words and/or things from the book they have just read. If they are able to attend a bit more, then pair students up and have them reread the book(s) you have been working with. You are now free to visit the background group.

You can assess two students in the background group daily using an anecdotal record notebook. This is a three-ring notebook that has lined paper in it. Put pieces of masking tape on pages to make a section for each of your students. Write their names on the pieces of tape.

If the background group is working with a reading box you can sit by one child and ask him/her things such as:

What is this sight word?
Can you find the word "said" on this page?
I will read this page and you point to the words while I read.
Please read this page to me.
Where is the letter "M"?
Tell me what is happening in the picture.
Read me an item from the box.
ETC.

This list is endless! Look at all the information you can get in a very short period of time; literally, in a couple of minutes. Write the information in your notebook and move on to the second child. You can usually assess two students every day.

If the background group is working with a discussion box, then you can sit with the whole group and ask some key questions to determine whether or not they comprehend the main idea and most important details in that reading assignment. You can also check on knowledge of vocabulary words or anything that may be confusing to them.

Overview of Part 1

	First	Next	Then	Last
Teacher	Calls two reading groups.	Works with the "front" group in a guided reading lesson.	After 20 minutes gives the guided reading group some clay or a reading assignment to be done at the table.	Assesses two students in the background group.
Front Group	Meets at the guided reading table when called by the teacher.	Works with teacher in a guided reading format.	After 20 minutes either makes letters, words, or things from the book out of clay. May read with a partner.	All clean up and begin independent work.
Background Group Reading Boxes	Meets on the floor or at a table in close proximity to the teacher.	Reader of the Day gets the reading box and begins with a read-aloud.	The read-aloud students all read silently.	Two students are assessed by teacher. All clean up and begin independent work.
Background Group Literature Discussion Boxes	Meets on the floor or at a table in close proximity to the teacher.	Each student is in charge of a certain discussion. Cubes are used as a management tool.	Continue discussions.	Two students are assessed by teacher. All clean up and begin independent work.

Part 2

What Are the Other Students Doing While I Am With a Guided Reading Group?

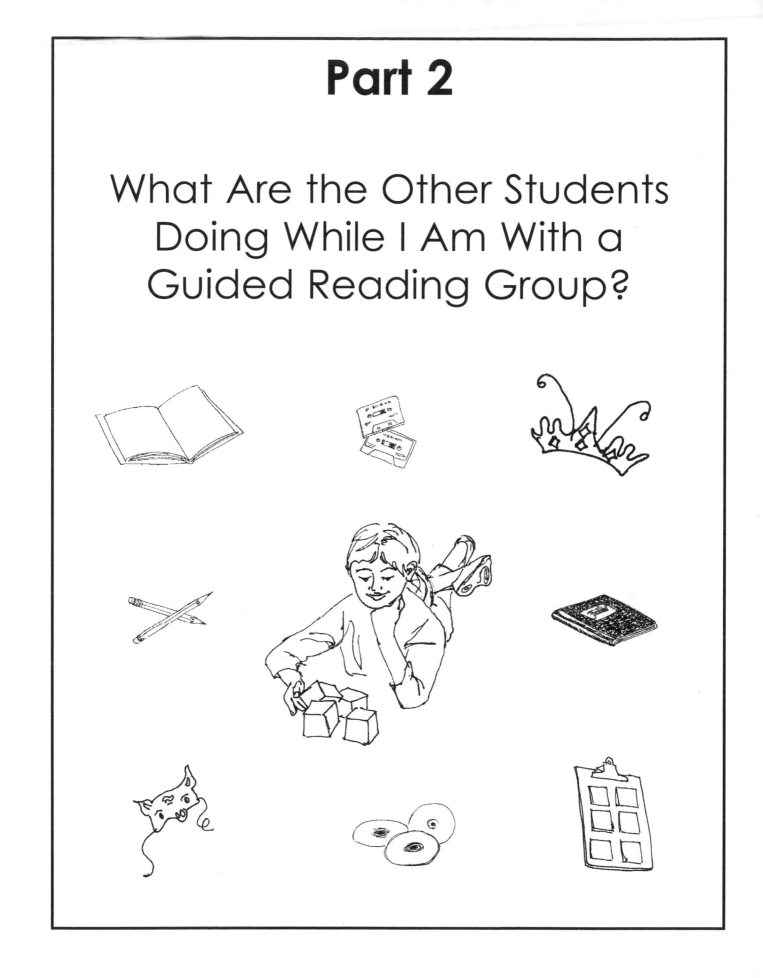

What is everyone else doing while I am with a guided reading group?

This question can make or break any kind of grouping situation. Students need to be actively engaged in meaningful assignments at their ability levels. If assignments are too hard, you have the "I don't get it" line that forms at your guided reading table. If assignments are too easy you hear, "I'm done. Now what do I do?"

There are two kinds of assignments to think about. The first kind of assignment is the work students do at their seats with workbooks, worksheets, new skills, etc. They are often whole class assignments where everyone gets the same work to complete. They usually include new directions that change per page or on a daily basis.

When working with these kinds of assignments the teacher needs to be accessible for questions. These assignments are often not multi-leveled, so they will be too hard for some and too easy for others. You need to be available to help those who need support; and challenge those who need enrichment.

The second kind of assignments are those given to students while the teacher is with a guided reading group and not available for help. These assignments need to be multi-leveled so that different ability levels can successfully complete the tasks. They need to be tasks that can be applied to any book and/or any skill.

The tasks and directions need to be consistent. Students will know how and what to do with the assignments because they are consistent all year. What changes each week is how the students apply and utilize learned skills with these assignments. Part 2 focuses on these types of assignments.

Building Foundations

Foundations support everything that is built upon them.

A lighthouse cannot lead and guide if it does not have a solid foundation which cannot be seen.

In a classroom, part of the foundation is students knowing how to work independently while the teacher is with a group. They need to know what to do when they get stuck or when they complete their work.

Modeling

One of the biggest mistakes in the classroom has been not building a strong enough foundation. Teachers show students how to do something once and then expect them to complete the assignment correctly. This usually does not happen.

Modeling plays an integral part in how successfully and easily students are able to complete assignments. Any assignment students are asked to complete while the teacher is with a group must be significantly modeled a number of times in a number of different ways.

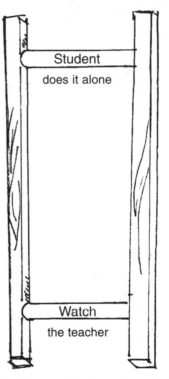

Think of a ladder.

Your goal is to get students to the top rung of the ladder.

The old paradigm might look like the ladder to the right.

There is too much distance for students to reach from the bottom rung all the way to the top rung. They will probably fall.

In the classroom, the "falling" may be these:

students interrupting the guided reading group,

students just sitting and not getting the work done,

students walking around the room,

behavior problems.

You need to give students support so they can and will make it to the top rung. The modeling now looks like this:

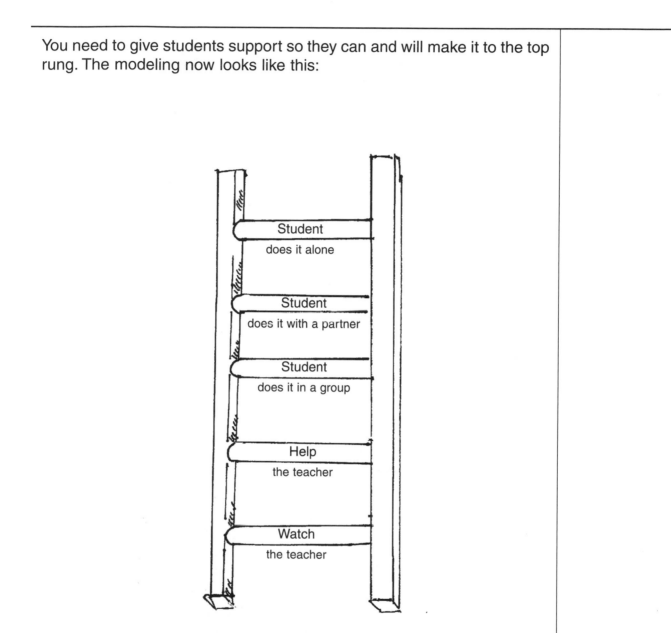

Student
does it alone

Student
does it with a partner

Student
does it in a group

Help
the teacher

Watch
the teacher

During guided reading instruction you want the least amount of interruptions possible, so any assignment given during this time should be modeled in the above way.

As you use this ladder as a basis for your modeling, keep in mind you may skip one rung if you feel students are grasping quickly, but never skip more than one rung.

Remember that the assignments being modeled are assignments that students will be using all year, so the foundation you are building will support your classroom management for the year.

Assignment Categories

This section gives a wealth of assignments that can be given to students while guided reading groups are in session. These assignments are organized into six different categories. Beaker, a real-life Amazon parrot whose picture is on the inside of the back cover, will be introducing each category. On the side of each activity page will be an icon of Beaker. The icon will tell you which category will be addressed while students are working through the specific assignment.

Writing

Students are often given assignments such as writing stories, describing characters, telling about the books they've read, etc. These tasks require students to "put it all together" and create an organized piece of writing. Students need lots of practice with simple, short tasks before moving onto more connected pieces of writing. The more students practice labeling, writing lists, describing items, etc., the easier the longer pieces of writing become. The more students write, the better writers they become.

Some of the assignments in this category are short, easy tasks that get children generating words and beginning to put something down on paper. Other tasks are more detailed and require more from students. Most of the activities are multi-leveled so that students of different abilities can successfully complete them. For some activities, there will be assignments for beginning writers as well as for fluent writers.

Listening

The listening center provides opportunities for students to listen to favorite stories, build fluency, gain confidence, and practice oral reading.

Literature Connections

These assignments can be used with any story or book students are working with. They can be stories from your guided reading groups or from a whole group read aloud. These activities range in variety from writing to art.

Phonics, Spelling, and Related Skills

Beaker is holding pieces of a puzzle to represent this category. The suggestions here will be general ideas. Use these ideas to reinforce and practice your specific content for the week or to review concepts already taught. Your curriculum will dictate specific assignments.

Sight Vocabulary

These high frequency words do not follow the typical phonetic rules. They do not represent spelling patterns. One of the keys to sight vocabulary acquisition is multiple exposures. Many of these assignments have students finding, making, reading, and writing the words over and over again. Activities in this category will reinforce reading and writing sight vocabulary.

Additional Activities

These activities include reading, writing, content areas, and art.

Writing Activities

If you already did it do it again more creatively

Top Ten

Make a chart like the example below. Using the same prompt each week, Top Ten_____, have students list their top ten:

Animals
Friends
Things that are green, red, yellow, etc. *blue*
Favorite foods
Sports
Things to do at recess
Favorite foods
Foods I do not like

Each week the only change to this assignment or center is the topic of the list. Laminate this chart and then each week all you need to do is wipe off the old topic and write in the new.

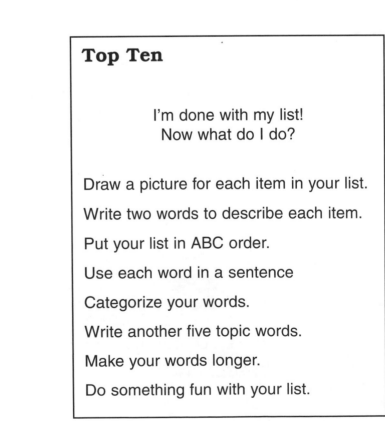

Top Ten

I'm done with my list!
Now what do I do?

Draw a picture for each item in your list.

Write two words to describe each item.

Put your list in ABC order.

Use each word in a sentence

Categorize your words.

Write another five topic words.

Make your words longer.

Do something fun with your list.

When students have completed their lists, they may choose any of the extensions listed on the chart. I used to have a fill-in form for students to use with this activity, but found that just lined or unlined paper can be used. It saves you time from having to copy the form and putting it at the center. It also requires that students take more ownership in choosing paper and setting it up.

You can tie this activity to any of your curriculum areas:

Science

things that are living
things that are non-living
places that are dark
kinds of weather
transportation
things on a farm
zoo animals
pets
things that float
things that a magnet attracts
things with wheels
things that move
baby animal names
things in space
things that live in the ocean
things that are sweet, sour, salty, etc.
things that grow
things that hatch

Math

things that are round, square, etc.
things that come in twos, threes, etc.
things that are bigger than a coffee can
things that are smaller than a coffee can
things that are longer than a foot (12")
things that are shorter than a foot (12")
things that can be cut exactly in half
ways to make the number 3,4,5, etc.
    (addition /subtraction facts)
ways to make $1.25
things that come in 6's or 12's (half-dozen or dozen)

Language Arts

words to describe a character
words to describe a setting
verbs
nouns
adjectives
two-syllable words
one-syllable words
compound words
words instead of "said"
words instead of "nice"
pairs of synonyms (cellar/basement)
pairs of antonyms (happy/sad)
homophones

Tie in your spelling and phonics each week. Students write ten words that have the pattern, sound, rule, etc., that has been studied during the week.

Social Studies

grocery list
items a fireman might need
items a policeman might need
things you find at the beach
differences between city and country
items in the kitchen, bedroom, etc.
things in your community
community helpers
things you see in the spring, summer, fall, winter
things in a post office
ocean words
ways to travel
things found on a map

Magazine Pictures, Calendar Pictures, and Posters

Laminate the pictures and posters. Students can write directly on the pictures and posters using overhead or dry erase markers. They can do any of the following suggestions depending on abilities:

label the beginning sound

label the beginning and ending sound

write the whole word

write a phrase

write a complete sentence

write 2-3 sentences

create a story

Tie your reading and writing skills into the pictures.

For example:

verbs you see in the picture
* write out the past, present, and future forms of each verb
* add "ing" to each verb

nouns you see in the picture
* write three adjectives for each noun listed
* make each noun plural
* use all of the nouns in three sentences using commas to separate words in a series

write a conversation between two people or two objects
* use quotation marks
* choose words other than "said"

write three sentences about the picture using a contraction in each sentence.

Story Starter Pictures

Do the following activity with your whole class before introducing the students to the idea of using pictures to help them with topic choices.

Hold up a picture. Have students brainstorm all of the topics that could be written about just by looking at that one picture. Teach students to "dig below the surface." My students were looking at a picture of two birds in a tree with an autumn background. The first thing they all said was, "a story about birds." After that first idea the room was silent. No other topics were volunteered. We then began to "dig below the surface." What else does that picture make you think about?

friends
family
the happiest time in my life
vacations
sports
animals
summer
swimming
seasons

After brainstorming with the whole class, put six pictures around your room. Number each picture from one to six. Have students work in groups of 4-5. Each group will need some paper and one student in each group will act as recorder. Each group will begin with a particular picture. The recorder will write the number of the picture on the top of the paper. Set a timer for 1-2 minutes. Students must brainstorm as many topics as they can about the picture.

When the timer goes off, each group takes their list of topics and moves clockwise to the next picture. This procedure is repeated until all groups have visited all of the pictures. (The recorder must write the number of each picture on the top of each list of brainstormed ideas.)

Bring students back together. Hold up one picture. Each group takes a turn giving a topic suggestion. If any other groups have the same idea, they must all cross it out. Students learn that the more creative they become, chances are no one else will have that idea.

Squiggle of the Week

Create a squiggle in the middle of a piece of paper and make a copy for each child. Students take the squiggle, turn it into a picture and then write about it. The following are some examples of first grade squiggle creations and writing from co-teachers Pacifica Casserta and Megan Ragozzine.

Two llamas are sharing grass with ecarthe andthey love ecarthe and they want to marry.

Two llamas are sharing grass with each other and they love each other and they want to marry.

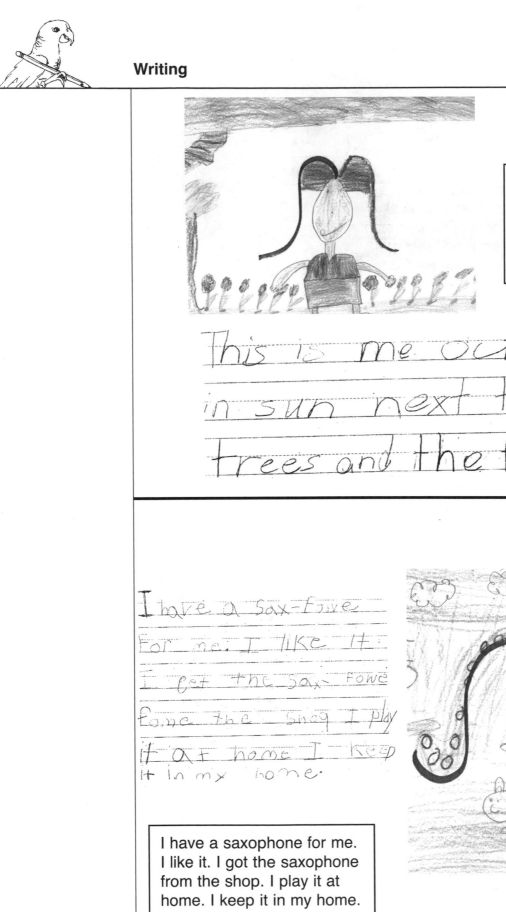

This is me outside in the sun next to the trees and the flower.

This is me outsite in sun next toth trees and the flower

I have a Sax-fowe For me. I like it. I got the Sax-fowe fome the shop I play it at home I keep it in my home.

I have a saxophone for me. I like it. I got the saxophone from the shop. I play it at home. I keep it in my home.

I made a map. A map is something that you use to go places that you have not been at before. That's why you need a map.

I made a map. A map is something that you use to go places that you have not been at before. That's why you need a map.

A girl and a boy are stuck in a castle and they don't know what to do. And it is a storm and they are scared.

A girl and a boy are stuck in casestrs and they don't know want to do. And it is a stone and they are scare.

Character Pictures

Students will write a story about a character from a guided reading book or a whole class read-aloud. They have two choices for creating a picture of the character.

Option One

Students are given a picture of a character to color, cut out, and glue onto a piece of drawing paper. They put the character into a scene by adding their own background, other characters, setting, etc. The pictures of the characters may come from pattern books, reproducibles, or coloring books.

Option Two

Students may draw their own character directly onto the piece of drawing paper. They put the character into a scene by adding their own background, other characters, setting, etc.

CLIFFGRD IS IN THE BEH OF HAYE.
I LEAK CLFFRD
CLFFRD IS The KAG
OF The BEH

Clifford is in the beach of Hawaii. I like Clifford. Clifford is the king of the beach.

He is in a band. I am playing drumsticks. Clifford is writing a
song.

HE SS MIA PNO I M PLANA DRM
SSDKS
CLFFID SS RIDN A SAN.

The Cat in the Hat
had lots of tricks to
show the kids

The cat in the hat had lots of
tricks to show the kids.

Some characters from books for fluent readers that I have used
include *Flat Stanley, Cam Jansen,* characters from *James and
the Giant Peach,* and characters from *Charlie and the Chocolate
Factory.*

Letters and Notes

Each week put up the name of a student in the classroom. Everyone has to write a letter to that student. Younger children usually write Dear _____, draw a picture and close with From or Love, _____.

Older children are given more direction. They must include three things in the letter.
1. Something they like about the student
2. Something positive they noticed about the student
3. Something they hope to do with the student
    before the year is over.

Keep these letters and bind each child's letters together. On Valentine's Day students are given a book of letters written to them by classmates.

After we had gone through all of the names in my classroom, this activity became open-ended. Students could write to anyone they wished. They had a difficult time with it being so general and always asked to whom they could write. So each week, for the rest of the school year, I put up a name of someone involved with our school. For example:

the principal
the nurse
the secretary
bus drivers
kitchen help
custodians
crossing guards
other teachers

The following are some examples of letters students have written to some of their friends and me.

DEAR LISA
HARV R YOU'DUN
Y+D YOU GAtFOR
SACM
IOUE

Dear Lisa,
How are you doing? What did you get for snacktime?

DeR MRs. CR

MY FAVit SiTR

iS WEDINt GOAMS.

i LoK to DoW PoZLs.
+DROi PiTHAS

Love CHRISTOPHER

Dear Mrs. Couture,

My favorite center is writing and games. I like to do puzzles and draw pictures.

Love, Christopher

Dear Lindsay,

My favorite color is purple. What is yours? I love you.

Love, Krystal

DEAR LINDSAY
ME FAVRET KALER iS PERPEL
WAT iS KERS I LOVE U
LOVE KRYSTAL

I'm going to Write a note to Mrses P.
Here I go!
Dear Misses P.
I like Scool
a lot. But I'm
glad That it is
allmost vacasin
Becaase I get
to go swim-
ing at My
grandfather's
lake. And I get
to see My
Cusins a lot
mare. But I Still
like scool a
holle bunch

I'm going to write a note to Miss P. Here I go! Dear Miss P. I like school a lot but I'm glad that it is almost vacation because I get to go swimming at my grandfather's lake. And I get to see my cousins a lot more, but I still like school a whole bunch.

Dear Kate,

This is from Ashley. There is a pumpkin in the cake.

Love, Ashley

The book *The Jolly Postman* by Janet and Allan Ahlberg is a great resource to use with letter writing. This book is about a postman who delivers letters to fairy tale characters. Every other page in the book is an envelope with a letter inside.

Students make their own "envelope book." They take three or four envelopes and staple them together. Students address each envelope and put a note/letter inside.

You could leave this assignment open-ended and not give directions as to what to include in the envelopes. Or make this teacher-directed by giving specific requirements for each envelope; such as a business letter, friendly letter, postcard, advertisement, etc.

Journals

Journals used to be a whole class assignment during a specific time of the day. For 15 minutes all students wrote in their journals. Journals are now a part of assignments when I am with guided reading groups.

Stackable Trays

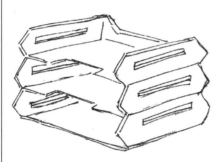

Stackable trays are plastic trays that stack on top of each other. In the trays are "fill-in" sheets for students to complete. Sometimes students have free choice as to which paper they want to do. Other times I assign a specific tray that they must complete first and then they have free choice. I usually have five to six trays available for students to choose from. Two excellent resources for stackable trays are *Making the Connection: Learning Skills Through Literature K-2* and *Making the Connection: Learning Skills Through Literature 3-6*.

Wordless Books

Wordless books are great resources to use to get children writing. I had a wealth of wordless books in my classroom that students were not really using, until I made the books manipulative and guided students a bit more. If you have access to a laminator, rip the books apart and send each page through the laminator. (Yes, it is hard to rip a book apart, but after the first tear it gets easier!) Cut the edges so they are even. Punch three holes in each page and tie them together with yarn. Using overhead markers, students can write directly on the pages of the books.

If you do not have a laminator, notebook sheet protectors will also work. (Yes, you still have to rip the book apart.) Cut the edges so they are even and put the pages into the sheet protectors. Most of the sheet protectors already have a strip with the three holes punched out. Put the sheet protectors into a three-ring notebook. (See the Appendix for a list of wordless books.)

Deep In The Forest by Brinton Turkle is a favorite for younger students. It is a take-off of Goldilocks and The Three Bears. Humans live in a house and decide to take a walk because their porridge is too hot, and a little bear comes into their house and creates havoc.

Zoom by Istvan Banyai is a wordless book that keeps students at the edge of their seats! It is a great book to use for predicting and looking at details. The first page is a zoom close-up of a rooster's comb. The second page is the rooster. As you turn each page the picture continues to move out and out and out...

Students can be given an assignment to go along with this book. Each student draws 3-4 pictures in the same zoom format as the book and then writes about the pictures. The following are examples from Kelley Auringer's third grade students at Hooker School in Bridgeport, Connecticut.

1

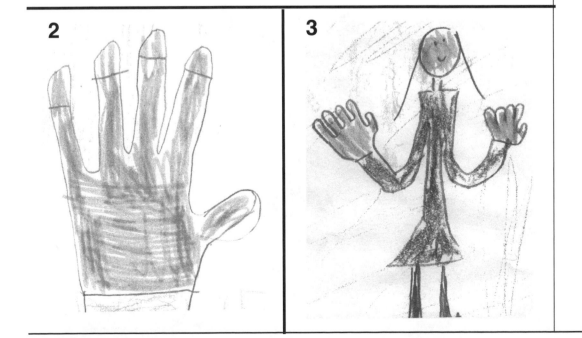

2

3

Writing

78

Authors

Students write books and stories. Some students will write a sentence or two about a topic and call it a "story," as shown in the examples below. Others may write a multi-page sequential story as shown on the following page. Students may be given a topic or choose a topic of their own.

> I have a dog at home. My dog's name is Libby.

> I have four pets: Cinnamon, Soot, Woody, Spike.

Baseball

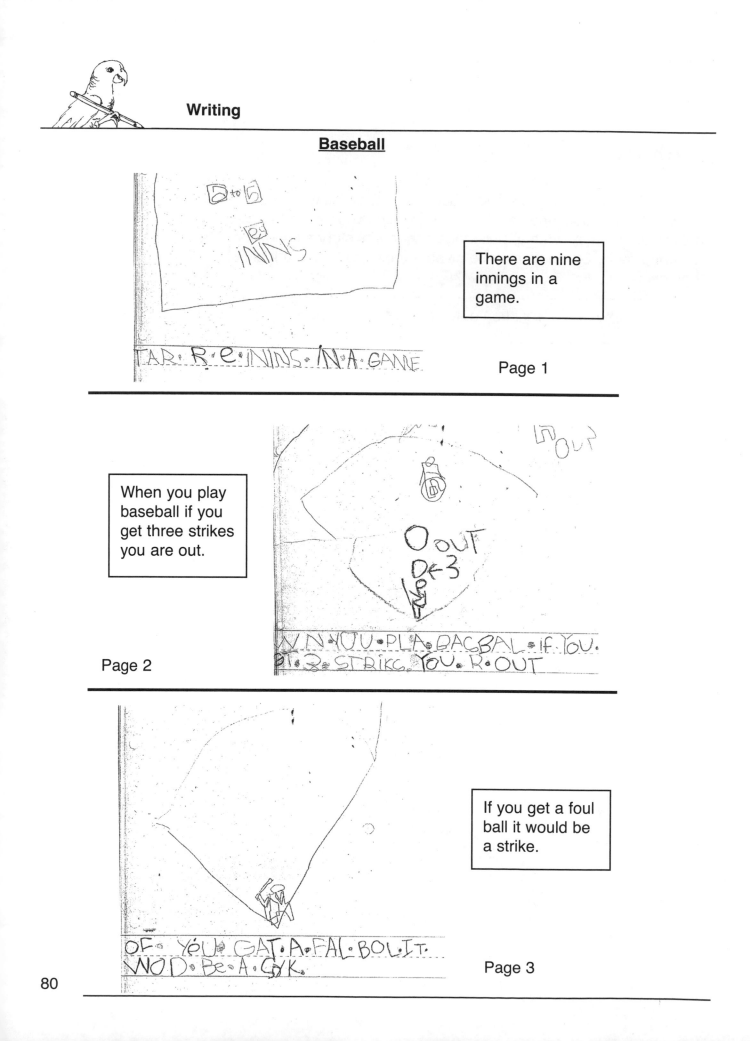

There are nine innings in a game.

TAR R e ININS IN A GAME

Page 1

When you play baseball if you get three strikes you are out.

Page 2

WN YOU PLA BACBAL if YOU GT 3 STRIKC YOU R OUT

If you get a foul ball it would be a strike.

OF YOU GAT A FAL BOL IT WOD BE A CYK.

Page 3

Listening Activities

Listening Station

The listening center provides opportunities for independent listening activities. After my students listened to a story, I always had a fill-in sheet for them to complete. The worksheet asked many questions about many different story elements. Students did a rather poor job filling in the sheets. They would often write: "I liked it" or "It was nice." I realized the sheets were too cumbersome and too general. Students also stated that they did not like having to fill out the same form each week after listening to a story.

I now take one story element each week and use it as a focus in the listening center. There is no fill-in available for students. Each week, depending upon the focus, students have activities from which to choose. The following are activities students can do at the listening center as you concentrate on different story elements.

Follow-Up Activities With Story Elements

Answers can be drawn, written, or a combination of the two.

Characters

Draw the character.
Make a Venn diagram comparing and contrasting you
    and a character.
What problems did the character have
    and how did they get solved?
Describe the character.
What is your opinion of the character?
Do you know anyone like the character?
Make a mobile about the character.

Setting

Draw the setting
Describe the setting with your senses. What would you hear?
    See? Smell? Touch? Taste?
What places do you know that are like the story's setting?
What places do you know that are the opposite
    of the story's setting?
Create a new setting for the story. How might the story change
    because of the new setting?

Problem / Solution

What problems are the characters facing?
Have you ever had those problems or know someone who has?
What are two solutions you would suggest to solve
    the character's problems?
How were the problems solved in the story?

New Endings or New Adventures

Create a new ending to the story.
Create another chapter.
Give the characters another adventure that includes you.
Write a new story about the characters.

Opinions

What is your favorite part? Why?
What didn't you like about the story? Why?
Create a new book cover.
Why should someone read or listen to this story?
Create a book review.

Beginning, Middle, and End or Summary

Draw pictures of the beginning, middle, end.
Write about the beginning, middle, end.
Make an event map of first, next, then, last.

Other Fun Options For Students

Listen to:

Nature Sounds   Animal Sounds   Songs   Music

Record different people in the school reading a story.

Record parents reading and children saying their favorite part.

Record your read-alouds and their discussions.

Color code the buttons on the tape recorder to help students work
independently.

Green for PLAY
Red for STOP
Yellow for REWIND
Blue for RECORD

Literature Connections

Literary Friends

Literary Friends are friends from literature that come to visit the classroom. Hang up a picture of a character. The character leaves a letter for the students asking them to write to him/her. I used a cardboard mailbox and attached the character to the mailbox. Either the teacher writes back or an older grade level class can do the writing. The character stays for about a month, or as long as the interest is there.

Below are examples of letters my students have written to literary friends.

To Mouse from the book *If You Give A Mouse A Cookie* by Laura Numeroff

Dear Mouse,

I love cookies too.

Love,
Adam

Dear Mouse,
How are you doing? Where do yo live? Do you like cookies?
Love, Cormac

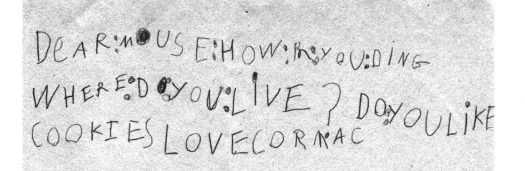

Dear Mouse,
Skye

To Ping from the book *The Story About Ping* by Majorie Flack.

Dear Ping,
Is it cold where you live?
Love, Krystal

DEAR PING
ISITCDELD WERU
LEU
LOVE KRYSTAl

DEAr PING WATRDOIN G LOV RYAN

Dear Ping,
What are you doing?
Love, Ryan

When you are ready to change the character, do it after school so the students are surprised the next morning. The character that goes away leaves cookies and a drink to say thank you to the students for writing to him/her, and a new character is on the mailbox.

My mom was a first grade teacher for twenty-eight years. She is a fabulous seamstress. She made this Clifford costume for us to use in the classroom. Clifford came to my classroom to personally thank the students for their letters and then he introduced the new literary friend.

Characters that have visited my classroom are *The Cat In The Hat, Clifford The Big Red Dog,* Max from *Where The Wild Things Are, Lovable Lyle,* and Ping from *The Story About Ping.*

Story Rewrites and Innovations

Text rewrites and innovations used in your classroom should go along with a read-aloud story or a book used during guided reading. Some students have a difficult time when given a blank piece of paper. My students are always given a "structure" to use for these assignments. The structure gives them a jump start to this writing assignment. Students do not have to use the structure. Below is an example of a structure for *I Was Walking Down the Road* by Sarah E. Barchas. Students need to fill in the end of the story.

I was looking for my coat.
Then I saw a little goat.

I was jumping on the rocks.
Then I saw some crocs.

Below is an example of a poem rewrite for "The Itsy Bitsy Spider."

THE jtsy - Bitsy spi der Welt UP-A-PUEC uV WOD He Lust FOR FODD BUT FAND NO FODD!

The Itsy Bitsy Spider went up a piece of wood. He looked for food but found no food.

Flipbooks

Flipbooks are made with any sized piece of paper.

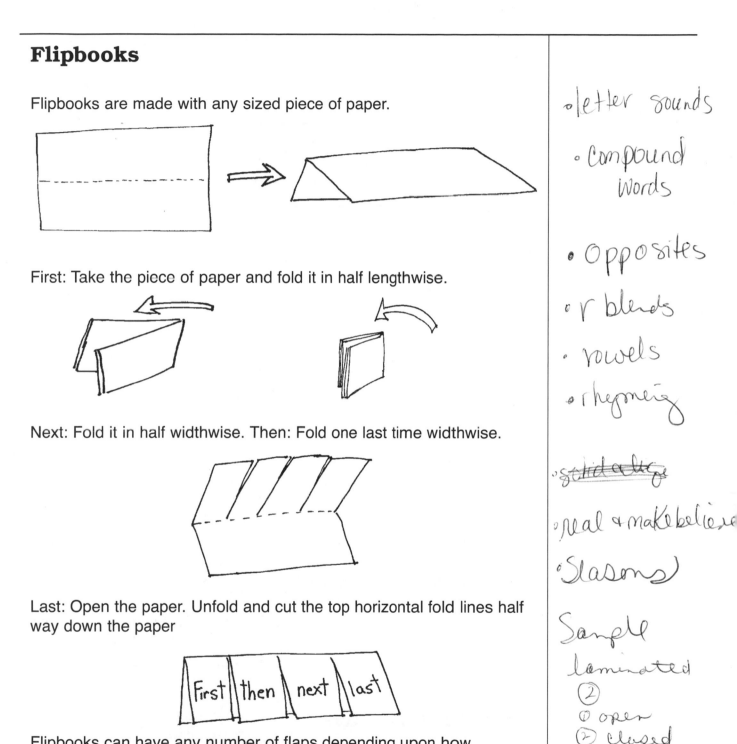

First: Take the piece of paper and fold it in half lengthwise.

Next: Fold it in half widthwise. Then: Fold one last time widthwise.

Last: Open the paper. Unfold and cut the top horizontal fold lines half way down the paper

Flipbooks can have any number of flaps depending upon how they are folded. They can be used for a number of different literature connection activities.

Sequencing

Students draw and/or write under each flap when retelling a story in proper sequence.

Summary

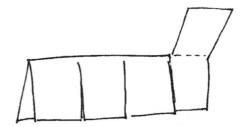

Students draw and/or write a summary of the story under each flap.

Story Elements

Students draw a picture on the top half of the page and write about the story element on the bottom half of the page.

Question Words

Who, What, Where, Why, When, How

Students make their flipbooks into six sections. They write the question words on the outside of the flipbooks. Students tell about these question words in relation to the story and draw pictures under the flaps.

Describing Characters

Students list four words to describe their character on the outside flaps.

They must back up their descriptions with evidence from the story. They may draw pictures, write down the evidence, or give pages numbers where the evidence is found in the book.

Students' Opinions About the Book

Students write four words that describe their feelings about the book on the outside flaps.

They must back up their opinions with evidence from the story. Students need to tell why they have those opinions.

Cause/Effect

Students write the cause on the outside of the flipbook and the effect on the inside of the book.

This activity works great with Laura Numeroff's books *If You Give A Mouse A Cookie, If You Give A Moose A Muffin,* and *If You Give A Pig A Pancake.*

Main Idea/Supporting Details

Students write the main idea of what they have read on the outside of the flaps. On the inside they write the supporting details.

This works well when students are in chapter books or books that take two or three days to complete. Students would work on one flap a day.

Find It In A Book

This activity usually corresponds with your language arts curriculum for the week. Using highlighter tape, students find examples of the skills they have been taught during the week. Below are examples of some curriculum areas I have used.

Three Types of Sentences

Students can find and highlight:
one sentence that ends with a period,
one sentence that ends with an exclamation mark,
one sentence that ends with a question mark.

They need to write each sentence and tell why it uses that specific punctuation mark. Flipbooks are great recording sheets for this activity. On the outside flap students write the punctuation mark. On the top inside flap the students write what kind of mark it is and then copy the sentence from their books. On the inside bottom flap they tell why that mark was used.

Quotation Marks

Students can highlight everything that a character says. After finding all of the dialogue, have them write three original sentences that they think the character might say.

Capital Letters

Students find and highlight words that begin with capital letters. After finding words, they need to record and categorize them in a flipbook. On the outside of the flipbook, students put the rule for capitalizing. For example: names of people, states, cities, streets, etc. On the inside they write the examples that were found in their books.

Words Instead of Said.

Find, highlight and record synonyms for the word "said."

These assignments allows students to actually see the skills embedded in context. It works well with most of our language arts skills.

Puppets

Students make puppets of the characters in a story. The puppets are then stored and used in the retelling station. Puppets are made out of small paper bags, paper plates, or socks. Have a box of supplies for students to use such as buttons, yarn, sequins, pom poms, bread tabs, pipe cleaners, glue, etc.

Below are examples of puppets some first graders made after listening to the story *Where The Wild Things Are* by Maurice Sendak.

These are the Wild Things!

Headband Masks

An alternative to puppets are headband masks. Students make the heads of characters on paper plates or out of construction paper. The heads are then stapled onto a headband so students can become the character.

Puppets and headbands are used in the retelling center which is explained on page 94.

Retelling

Retelling is a valuable instructional strategy. Retelling enhances oral language development as well as helps children practice sophisticated language structures. Students are actively involved with reconstructing the story and organizing the sequence. Retelling can increase students' comprehension.

Props for retelling can include:

1. Feltboards and Figures

Individual feltboards can be made by taking 12" by 18" pieces of cardboard and covering them with felt. Group feltboards can be made by using larger pieces of cardboard. Students retell stories by manipulating felt figures on the feltboards. Below is a picture of pieces from the story *Three Billy Goats Gruff*.

2. Puppets

See page 93 for information about puppets.

3. Headband Masks

See page 93 for information about headbands.

4. Storyboards

Storyboards are made with paper bags. There is no particular way to make storyboards. Bags can be cut and made into different shapes. Paper can be stapled onto the bags. The bags can be used as is.

Students draw the setting(s) on the bag. If the story has one setting, then students draw one setting on the bag. If there are more settings, different sides of the bag can be used for each setting or paper can be stapled onto the bag. Below is an example of a storyboard for the book *Goldilocks and the Three Bears.*

While working with teachers we brainstormed and created samples of storyboards for our classrooms. Below are examples of our creations.

Phonics, Spelling, and Related Skills

Playing With Words

The following is made from a three-fold presentation board.

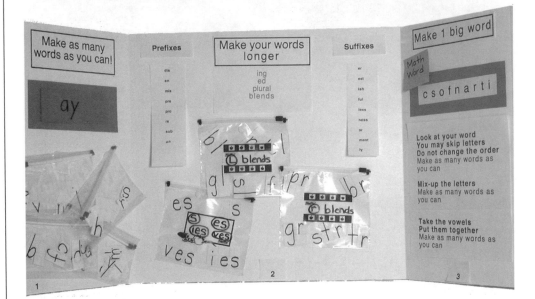

Preparation For Section 1

Baggies

Fill six small baggies with consonants. Consonants can be written on 1" by 1" graph paper and then run off and put into each bag. Put in extra copies of the popular consonants such as R,S,T, etc. Velcro these baggies to the board.

Text

Write the following along the top of this section: **Make as many words as you can.** Laminate a piece of red paper about 3" by 8". Tape it to the board directly under the title. This is where you will write the pattern students are to work with each week.

Other Materials

Place a margarine tub filled with strips of red paper next to the board.

Section 1

The goal of this section is to have students make as many words as they can with the pattern being studied during the week. The pattern is in red at the top of the board.

Students take a piece of red paper from the margarine tub and copy the pattern that is in red on the board.

They take a baggy of letters off the board. Keeping the red pattern consistent, students make as many word as they can by changing the beginning and ending consonants. They must record all the words they make.

If students get done before work time is over they can do the following: draw pictures about their words, use the words in sentences, or go on to the second section of the board.

Preparation For Section 2

Baggies

Fill some small baggies with "add-ons." These can be written on 1" by 1" graph paper and then run off and put into each bag. The following are suggestions for these baggies.

Suffixes	Prefixes	"L" Blends	"R" Blends
ing	pre	bl	br
ed	re	cl	fr
ly	mis	fl	gr

Text

Write the following along the top of this section: **Make your words longer.**

Section Two

The goal of this section is to have students make their words longer. Using the words created in section one, students add suffixes, prefixes, blends, etc.

As you teach different endings, put them on the board for students to practice using. The first endings I usually put up are "ing", "ed", and "s". As students continue to learn more throughout the year, make baggies to Velcro onto the board. For example: "es", change the "y" to "i" and add "es", "er", etc.

If students were working with "ay", and made the word "pay" in section one, then the following changes could be made in section two:

Using the Suffix Baggie

Paying   Pays
Payment   Payer

Using the Prefix Baggie

Prepay

This is just a small sampling of the different ways to play with the word "pay." They must record all the words they make. If students get done before work time is over they can do the following: draw pictures about their words, use the words in sentences, or go on to the third section of the board.

Preparation For Section 3

Text

Write the following along the top of this section: **Make one big word.**
Write a scrambled word on red paper for this section. It is always a
curriculum word from math, science, or social studies. Place a post-it
next to the scrambled word telling what content area it is from.

Other Materials

Place a coffee can filled with strips of 1" graph paper next to the
board.

Section 3

Students take a strip of graph paper. They copy the letters from the
red strip on the board onto their graph paper. Students then cut the
graph paper apart and unscramble the letters to make one long
content word. I find this activity becomes too hard if the scrambled
word is not one that they have been working with in the classroom.
Putting a post-it near the scrambled word telling what content area it is
from is also very supportive for students. For example:

r t n o s a f c i

They know it is a math word because of the post-it. First, students
unscramble the word and write it on a piece of paper.

fractions

Then students make as many words as they can using any one of the
three options on the following page.

Option 1

Look at your word.
You may skip letters.
Do not change the order.
Make as many words as you can.

Fractions

in	tin	fin	fins
at	rat	rats	fat
on	ton	tons	an
fan	fans	ran	act

This is a sampling of the words that can be made.

Option 2

Take the vowels.
Which pairs would go together?
Make as many words as you can.

Fractions

A I O

AI	Students make as many "ai" words as they can.
OA	Students make as many "oa" words as they can.
OI	Students make as many "oi" words as they can.

Option 3

Mix-up the letters.
Make as many words as you can.

F r a c t i o n s

coin	coins	tar	train
rain	rains	star	cart

This is a sampling of the words that can be made.

Pull-Throughs and Flip-Overs

Below is an example of a pull-through. Students pull the strip of paper and make words containing the "ark" pattern.

Below is an example of a flip-over. Students flip over the paper on the left to make words containing the "in" pattern.

 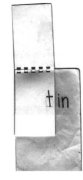

Pull-throughs and flip-overs directly coordinate with your phonics and spelling patterns. Students have four tasks with each word they make.

1. Read the word.

2. Write the word.

3. Draw the word.

4. Use the word in a sentence.

Story paper with the lines on the bottom and plain top for a picture is a great resource to use with this assignment.

Walking the Room

Students can complete this activity either individually or with a partner. Write vowel patterns, blends, etc. on post-it notes and place on clipboards.

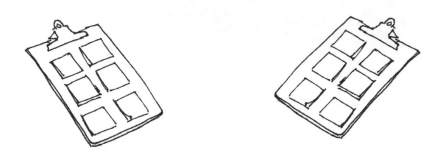

The first time students walk the room they place the notes on words that contain the pattern, blend, rule, etc. The second time students walk the room they take off the post-it notes and copy the sentences in which the words were found.

Students then go back to their seats and use each word in their own sentences.

Extensions

Any of the following can be put on post-its for students to find around the room.

Letters of the Alphabet
Sight Words
Contractions
Plurals
Words with "ing" ending
Quotation Marks
Parts of speech: nouns, verbs, adjectives, adverbs
Capital Letters
Color Words

Sight Vocabulary

Find It and Mark It Again and Again

Have students work with a sight word. Using any book, they need to find and mark the word every time it appears in the text. Depending on abilities, students can work with just one word or up to four words.

The first time through the book students mark the sight word every time it appears. The second time through the book students read the book and take off the tape as they come to the word. The following items can be used to mark the words.

Highlighter Tape

See page 30 for information about highlighter tape.

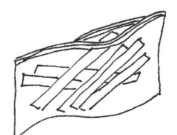

Post-Its

Students put a post-it under the word every time they see it. I use the square post-its, cut them into strips and store them in Ziploc baggies.

Arrows

Arrows are like highlighter tape because they can be reused. Arrows can be found at most office supply stores. Store these on strips of laminated paper like the highlighter tape.

Wikki Stixs

These are colored stixs that are reusable. Students shape them into circles to circle the words or leave them in strips to underline the words. These can be stored in a margarine tub.

Write a Sentence

Use the book *Look-Alikes* or *Look-Alikes Jr.* by Joan Steiner to set up and organize this activity. The pictures in these two books are made from household objects and items. For example, the roof of a house is really a book. The chimney is made of dog bones. The trees are broccoli. The porch is made out of birthday candles. It is a clever and motivating book. Put one copy of this book in an area. Clothespin the book open to the pages you want your students to use. Give them a different prompt each week. The prompt is a sentence that contains high frequency words. It should be no longer than four words. Some examples of prompts I've used are:

Look at the ___.
I see a ___.
I see the ___.
Here is a ___.
Here is the ___.
I saw a ___.
There is a ___.
I found a ___.
It was a ___.

Some of my students have written the sentence over 10 times because they love finding the objects in the book.

You can make the prompts harder for those who want some challenges. For example:

I found a ___ used as a ___.
This is a ___ used for a ___.
You could have used a ___ instead of a ___.
You really wouldn't find a ___ used as a ___.
I noticed a ___ used for a ___.

This could also be used as a dictionary center. Students need to check the words they have independently written.

Going, Going, Gone

Students can work with a partner or in a small group. They need to use a large classroom blackboard or small portable chalkboards. One child takes a damp sponge and writes a sight word on the board. The other students have to say and spell the word as many times as they can before it disappears. When it finally disappears they all have to write it on a piece of paper. The word is then rewritten on the board with the sponge and students correct their work. Write sight words on index cards and keep them in a coffee can. The student with the sponge uses the cards to choose and spell the words.

Clay or Playdough

Students make the word(s) out of clay or playdough at least three times. Have them leave their words in a tray for you to check. Use styrofoam trays that contained family-sized portions of meat from the grocery store. After students have made their word(s) at least three times they have free play with the playdough or clay.

Sand or Salt Trays

Using large styrofoam trays, fill some with sand or salt. Students write sight words in the sand or salt, and then write it with paper and pencil. Place the trays in a plastic tub to help contain the salt and sand.

Sentence Cubes

This assignment reinforces sentence structure, sight words, and punctuation. Make four cubes using the pattern on page 149. On each cube write the following words or use your own ideas.

Cube #1	Cube #2	Cube #3	Cube #4
My	dog	walked	to the store.
His	mom	went	home.
Their	dad	drove	to the beach.
Our	cat	rode	to the park.
Her	friend	came	to school.
Your	brother	raced	to the mall.

Cube #1 has pronouns.

Cube # 2 has any animal name, family member name, or the word friend.

Cube #3 has verbs.

Cube #4 has places.

Assemble cubes as explained on page 46.

The assignment is to roll the cubes, write the sentence and then illustrate. Students usually roll the cubes a couple of times before they write the sentence. They can make a little book using the pattern on page 150. Run many copies, cut them in half, and let students assemble their own mini books. Students may take only four pages at a time. You might have students write the four sentences first before beginning their drawings. This is an individual activity. It may be difficult for students to do this in pairs or groups because of the "throwing" of the cubes.

To make this more challenging, make some blank cubes. Students have to insert the cubes into the sentence to make the sentences longer. They need to add adjectives, adverbs, prepositional phrases, etc.

Color Words

The cubes can also be used for color words.

Cube #1
Every side has
the word "The"

Cube #2
Each side has
an animal name

Cube #3
Every side has
the word "is"

Cube #4
Each side has
a color word

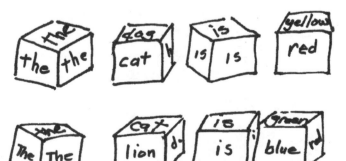

Below are two examples:

Our mother drove to the store.

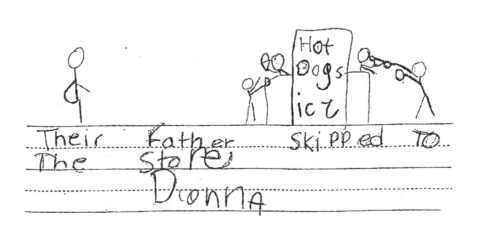

Their Father skipped to The store Donna

Additional Activities

Newspaper Detectives

Take a box and cover it with newspaper. Ask three or four students to volunteer for this job. They need to cut out different parts of the newspaper and glue them until the whole box is covered.

Punch two holes in a flap of the box. Tie a long piece of yarn to each hole. Put a brad on the back of the box. When you set up the box, pull the top up and attach both pieces of yarn to the brad. You have created a flap that will stand up. This is where you can put your focus skills or directions for the week. Put several newspapers in the box.

Below are two photos that show how the box can be used with younger and older students. The left photo is a newspaper box used in first grade. Students use the newspapers to find words they recognize which begin with the letter "A". Students cut out the words, glue them on a piece of paper, and then use the words in sentences.

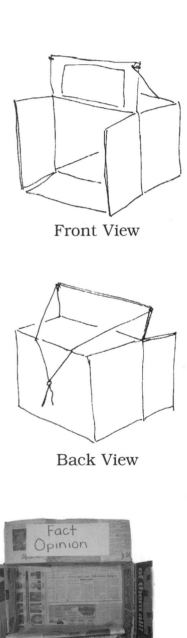

Front View

Back View

The box on the right can be used with third graders as they explore the difference between fact and opinion. Students read an article and write down the title on a piece of paper. They make a "T" chart and write down statements in the correct category: fact or opinion. See appendix for a reproducible that students can use.

Morning Message Station

Morning messages can be used over and over again all week for students to practice reading and writing. Each morning write a quick letter/message on chart paper to the students. A first or second grade example might look like the following:

Dear Students,

Good morning. I missed you this weekend.
We have library this afternoon.

Love,

Miss Pavelka

You will need a piece of clear plastic large enough to cover the letter. Run your laminating machine with nothing in it to get a large sheet of clear plastic. If you do not have access to a laminator then clear contact paper will also work. Put the sticky sides together to create a large sheet of plastic.

Each morning the students work as a class with the morning message; circling words they know and working with other reading and writing strategies. By putting the clear plastic over the chart paper, the letter can be used over and over again because it is not being written on. The writing, circling, etc. is done on the plastic which can be wiped off.

The letter is then placed at a morning message station. Students place the plastic over the messages and manipulate and play with the text. They often play "school." One is the teacher and tells the other students what to do with the letter. Children circle words they know, change the text, add descriptive words, etc.

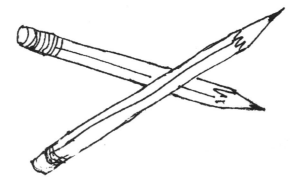

A third grade letter might look like the following:

Dear Third Graders:

I missed you this weekend.
Saturday I shopped and watched a movie.
Yesterday I baked cookies and helped some friends.
Today we go to art at 11:15.

　　　　Love,

　　　　Miss Pavelka

Third grade letters contain many examples of skills that they have been working on in the classroom. The above letter has words with the "ed" ending.

Students also practice writing their own morning messages.

These same activities can be done with language experience stories.

Mobiles

Mobiles are made using twigs and paper. Students bring the twigs in from recess. They should not be longer than 12".

Using paper strips of any size and color, students wrap the strips around the twigs and staple or tape them down.

While working with teachers, we brainstormed and created samples of mobiles for our classrooms. Below are some examples of our creations.

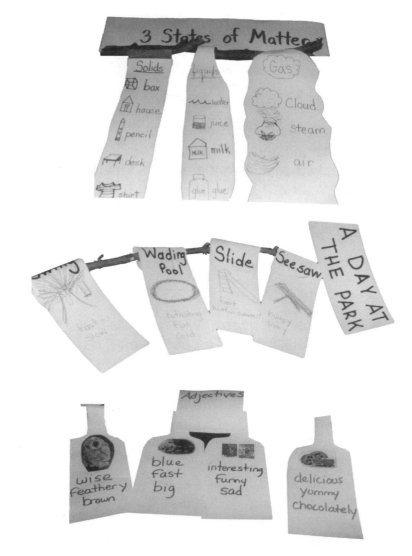

Mobiles can be used for all curriculum areas. Students can use magazine pictures and glue them on the strips. They can draw and/or write on the strips.

Part 3

Organizing and Scheduling Center Work and Assignments

Centers / Work Groups

**Students are in two groups:
a reading group and a center/work group.**

Center/work groups are heterogeneous groups of students working alone, or with each other as assignments and/or centers are being completed.

Guided reading groups are homogeneous groups of students working together with the teacher in a guided reading format or independently as a background group (see Part One). These are students who are reading at approximately the same level.

These two groups will be discussed individually and then in coordination with each other.

Each student is a member of a center/work group. They are called center or work groups because:

> * students work together in centers,
> > (They may all be doing individual tasks at the center, but they are physically there together.)
>
> > or
>
> * students may complete work independently at their seats.

Preparation for Center/Work Groups

Determining the Number of Centers Needed

The number of centers you need depends upon your class size. There should be no more than four students working together at one center at a time. The more centers you have, the easier they are to manage. Because there are fewer students working together or near each other, problems are kept to a minimum.

To determine the number of centers you need, take your class size and divide it by four.

For example:

20 - 22 students	You will need 5 centers
23 - 25 students	You will need 6 centers
26 - 28 students	You will need 7 centers
29 - 32 students	You will need 8 centers

Use the above figures as a general rule of thumb. You may decide that you want more or fewer centers.

Forming The Groups

Try to have a wide range of abilities and personalities in each group. For example, each group may have:

* a child who has difficulties with attention and behavior
* a calm child who has no difficulties with attention and behavior
* a proficient reader
* a struggling reader

You want these groups to be diverse in both personalities and learning styles.

These groups change membership only twice a year. You want to create a group of students that learns how to work together. They support each other in both academic and social areas. Once they have established a working relationship, you don't want to change them and begin the process all over. You may find when you first establish the groups, you might need to make some minor adjustments and move some students.

There are the same number of groups as there are centers. If you have five centers, there are five center/work groups. If you have six centers, there are six center/work groups, etc.

Each group has a color name: red, blue, green, yellow, etc. The teacher assigns each group a color.

Rotation Chart

Before making a rotation chart, you need to know how many centers you want (see page 117). You need two pieces of posterboard, one white and one of a light color. Use the light colored piece of posterboard as the background. Take the white piece of posterboard and cut out a large circle (wheel). Using a magic marker, divide the wheel into the number of centers needed. Color each section of the wheel a different color. Laminate the wheel.

Using a paper fastener, attach the wheel to the middle of the background posterboard. Continue the lines that divide the wheel onto the background posterboard with magic marker.

See the examples on the following page. (Remember your wheel sections are different colors. These examples are shown in black and white.)

Examples of rotation wheel using:

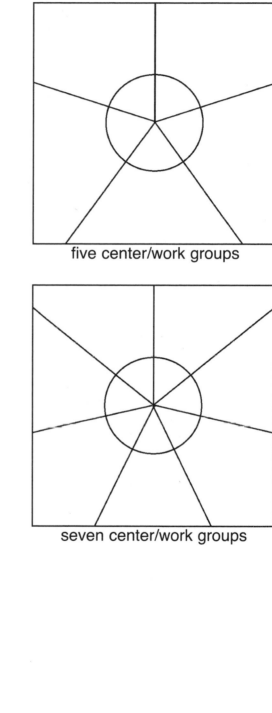

four center/work groups

five center/work groups

six center/work groups

seven center/work groups

eight center/work groups

Names of the students will be written in each color section of the wheel. Because the wheel is laminated you can change group memberships if the need arises and not have to make a new wheel. Names can be added, removed, or changed by just wiping off and rewriting. (Make sure you use overhead, non-permanent markers).

The background sections are for writing the different assignments and/or centers. See the example below of a "6 Activities" rotation chart.

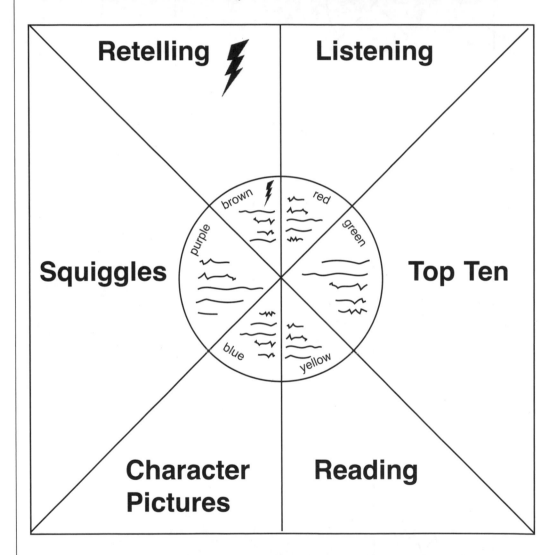

Put a sticker, symbol, etc., on one of the colored wheel sections and on one of the center assignments. In the above example, a lightning bolt is placed on the retelling center and the brown section of the wheel. Begin the wheel rotation with the two lightning bolts aligned together. As you turn the wheel the symbols become unaligned. When the lightening bolts realign, your students have completed one full rotation of centers.

Keep the center assignments the same for two rotations, not necessarily two weeks. Organizing centers in a Monday through Friday routine often leads to playing catch-up on Fridays. There is also little flexibility for students who are absent, pulled out for extra help, school cancellations, or special programs taking classroom time.

With a two-rotation routine you move the wheel when you come back from a school cancellation, holiday, or field trip. Also, students who have been absent or missed a center get a chance to revisit the center and complete the assignment.

As you organize your chart, be aware of the order of the centers. Try not to put two writing centers/activities next to each other, or two easier centers/activities next to each other. For example, you would not want to put wordless books next to text rewrites or cubes next to squiggles. (See Part 2 for descriptions of these assignments).

Getting Started Step by Step

Week I

Goals: **Students learn their color groups.**
Introduce two assignments from Part II.

Color Groups

Hang up your BLANK rotation chart. Do not have any names or centers written on it. Have students sit so they can easily see the rotation wheel. Write down the names of students onto the colored sections as they watch you. (See page 117 for information on how to establish the groups.)

Engage in quick activities all week long to help students learn their group colors. Have students line up for lunch, recess, art, music, library, gym, etc. by colors. Throughout the day ask different colored groups to do certain tasks. For example:

"Blue group, stand up."
"Green group, wave at me."
"Red group, put your hands in the air."

Assignments

Introduce two assignments to the students. Spend two days on each assignment and a review of both on Friday. Introduce these assignments to your whole class. Students do not know that these assignments will eventually be centers. Your goal is to teach these activities so that students will be able to work independently on them while you are with a guided reading group.

After introducing an assignment, have students sit in their color groups to complete the task. As they are working, you will be monitoring groups looking for strengths and weaknesses. Try not to answer any questions that may arise. Lead students to ask each other for help and clarification of directions. By having them work in their color groups, you will see how they interact and whether or not you need to do some movement of membership.

On Friday, write the names of the two assignments on the rotation chart. After week one, your chart may look like this:

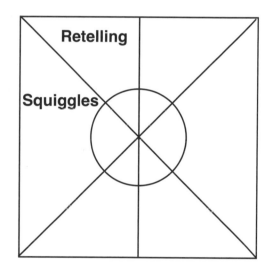

If students ask why you are writing the assignments on the chart, tell them they will find out soon! Trying to explain that they will be centers may lead to confusion.

Week II

Goals: **Students continue learning their color groups.
Introduce two more assignments from Part II.**

Color Groups

Continue working with students' knowledge of their color groups.
Engage in quick activities all week long to help students learn the colors of their groups. Have students line up for lunch, recess, art, music, library, gym, etc. by colors. This week you want to introduce movement to the groups. Throughout the week ask different colored groups to quickly and quietly walk to certain places in the classroom. For example:

"Blue group, walk quickly and quietly to the window."
"Green group, go quickly and quietly to the back of the room."
"Red group, walk quickly and quietly to the tall bookcase."

Your goal is to help students get from their desks or tables to certain places in the room in a quiet manner and as quickly as possible. (This is really practice for going to centers.)

Assignments

Introduce two more assignments from Part I to students. Follow the same format as week one:

        * introduce activities to the whole class,
        * spend two days on each assignment,
        * monitor groups for strengths, weaknesses and possible group
            changes,
        * guide students to ask each other for help and clarification,
        * review both assignments on Friday.

On Friday, write the names of the two learned center activities on the wheel rotation chart. After week two, your chart may look like this:

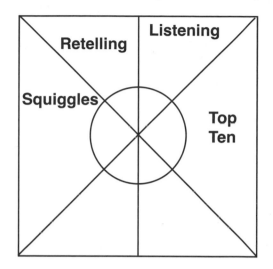

If students ask why you are writing the assignments on the chart tell them they will find out next week!

Week III

Goals: **Students learn how to understand the wheel rotation. Introduce two more assignments from Part 2.**

Color Groups and Rotation Chart

Students should now know what color groups they belong to. This week, you want to introduce the rotation chart. Have students find their colors on the wheel and then look at the activity that is next to their color. Rotate the wheel and have students find their color and the new assignment that is next to their color. Groups with no activity next to their color should be able to identify, "there is no activity by my color."

Turn the wheel at different times of the day and practice. For example, ask the group who would be working with the squiggle to stand up. Ask the blue group to tell what assignment is next to their color, etc.

Review directions to the assignments that are written on the chart.

Assignments

Introduce two more assignments from Part 1 to students. Follow the same format as weeks one and two.

On Friday write the names of the two learned center activities on the wheel rotation chart. After week three, your chart will be filled in and may look like this:

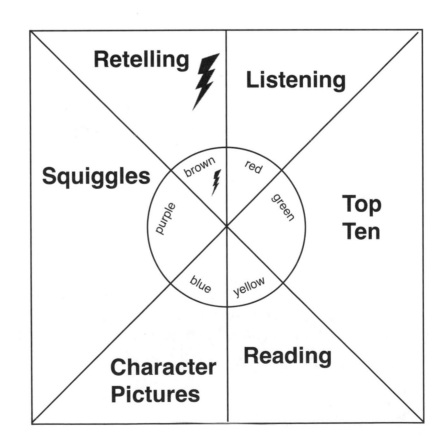

Week IV

Goals: **Set up centers with students**
Introduce new assignments if needed
(**six assignments have been introduced so far**)
Students read and apply the rotation chart
Coordinate the guided reading groups and center groups

Walk the room with your students, setting up the various centers and assignment stations. Students should help decide where directions are displayed, where materials are kept, etc.

Centers are places where students work either on the floor or at a table. They do not work at their seats.

Assignment or work stations are places where materials are kept. Students take the materials and work at their seats.

Most of the activities in Part 2 can be set up as either centers or assignment/work stations.

In this example of Getting Started Step by Step, a "6 Activity" rotation chart was used. It would take four weeks to establish the foundation.

If you want to work with a "7 Activity" or an "8 Activity" rotation chart, you may need to add one more week to establish your foundation.

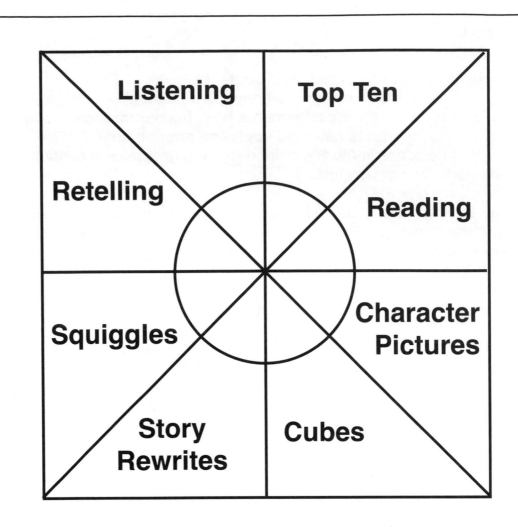

Set up each center in the order that it is on the rotation chart going clockwise. Using the "8 Activities" rotation chart above, you may organize your centers and work stations with students in this order:

Top Ten, Reading Center, Character Pictures, Cubes, Story Rewrites, Squiggles, Retelling Center, and finally Listening Center.

Take the first part of week five to organize and arrange your classroom centers and work stations. Use the last part of week five for students to practice finding their colors and walking to the corresponding center or work station.

Guided Reading Groups

Each student is also a member of a reading group that is at his/her instructional level. These are the groups discussed in Part I. When these groups meet, it is either with the teacher in a guided reading format or in the background working with reading boxes or literature discussion boxes.

The guided reading groups are flexible. Groups are changed approximately every month depending upon your assessments and the students' needs. There may be only a small amount of movement. You do not need to change all of the groups every four weeks. The changes are subtle.

Students may move to a group working with easier books or more challenging books, depending upon their needs. For example, if a student is having difficulty with fluency, move him/her to a group working with easier texts so fluency can be addressed. After the four weeks, you may move him/her back to his/her original level to see if there are improvements.

By moving just one to two students, the whole group dynamic changes! Groups do not become stagnant with the same students always working together. Each group has a least one new member who brings new ideas and personality.

Students need to see that you are moving them around to all different levels depending upon their needs at the time. Sometimes they will be working with easier texts. Sometimes they will be working with harder texts. When students see that groups are flexible and not the same for months on end, they lose that sense of "top group" and "bottom group" labels.

Each time new guided reading groups are formed, students give themselves a name based on a science or social studies theme being studied at that time. Calling groups by letters or numbers such as A,B,C, etc. or 1,2,3, etc. seems to make students more aware of levels. Even when arbitrarily assigning letters or numbers to groups, some students appear to be concerned about the levels. Letters were used in Part 1 of this book to explain the group rotations to make it easier for you to understand, but in the classroom with the students, different titles are used.

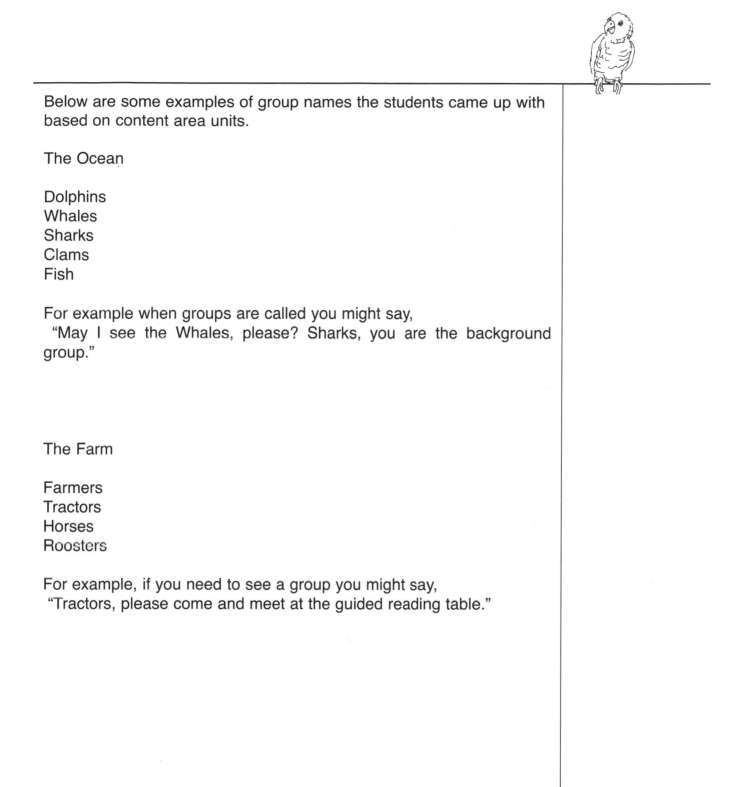

Below are some examples of group names the students came up with based on content area units.

The Ocean

Dolphins
Whales
Sharks
Clams
Fish

For example when groups are called you might say,
   "May I see the Whales, please? Sharks, you are the background group."

The Farm

Farmers
Tractors
Horses
Roosters

For example, if you need to see a group you might say,
   "Tractors, please come and meet at the guided reading table."

Coordinating Center/Work Groups with Guided Reading Groups

Preparation

Make two signs. Take a piece of 9" by 12" white construction paper and laminate it. Take a second piece of 9" by 12" white construction paper, draw a large red arrow in the middle of it, and laminate.

 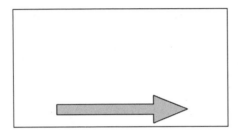

Practice with Students

On the blank laminated paper, use a water soluble, overhead marker to write the name of a guided reading group that you want to meet with. For example: hold up the sign below while you ask the Whales to meet with you at the guided reading table.

After the Whales come to you, the remaining students look at the rotation chart, find their colors, and go to the corresponding centers. When students have completed this task, ask them to sit down.

Hold up the sign again with a different guided reading group's name. For example: hold up the sign below while you ask the Sharks to meet you at the guided reading table.

Sharks

After the Sharks come to you, ask the remaining students to look at the chart, find their colors, and go to the corresponding centers. When students have done this task, ask them to sit down. Continue this procedure until all guided reading groups have practiced coming to you while the rest of the class finds their assignments.

You are not taking guided reading groups for instruction and students are not actually doing the center/work assignments. Students are practicing slow and quiet movement to centers or to you for instruction.

Students will miss the assigned center when they are working with you but they will have another opportunity to do the assignment because the center/work assignments are a two-week rotation.

You are now ready to begin implementing guided reading instruction because you have created a solid foundation for students working independently at centers or at their seats!

Coordinating Center/Work Groups, Guided Reading Groups, and Background Groups

Background groups are not explained whole class. During the first five minutes that each guided reading group meets, begin setting up and explaining background group tasks. Organize the box of reading materials with students. Make the highlighter tape cards and index cards with students. Have students help you organize and set up the box as much as possible. The more involved they are in the foundation, the greater their ability to understand the given tasks and complete them independently.

Practice the Reader of the Day activities, sitting on the circles, reading silently, etc. When you think students are ready to work independently as a background group, put them in the background and observe instead of taking them for a guided reading lesson,.

When all groups understand background group assignments and responsibilities, spend a couple of days practicing the movement of all three groups: guided reading groups, center/work groups, and background groups. Follow the same procedure as week four. Now you will need both pieces of laminated paper; the blank one to write down the name of a group for guided reading and the paper with the arrow to write down the name of the background group. The arrow points the background group to its work area.

Using the example below you would ask the Whales to meet you at the reading table, the Sharks to meet as a background group, and everyone else to work on their color group assignment. (Write "Sharks" on the laminated 9 X 12 paper that has the arrow on it. The arrow leads the Sharks to their background group meeting area).

All three groups change approximately every 20 minutes. In one hour all students would have:

1.   Worked with a center or work assignment for 20 minutes
2.   Worked with a second center or work assignment
        for 20 minutes
3.   Worked with the teacher in a guided reading format
        or worked in a background group format
        for 20 minutes

In this example there are:

    6 center/work groups
    5 guided reading groups

Students come from all different centers. Notice that you can start with five in a center because when you call for groups, the number of students that remain in the center drops by one or two.

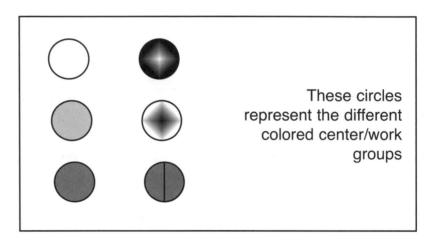

These circles represent the different colored center/work groups

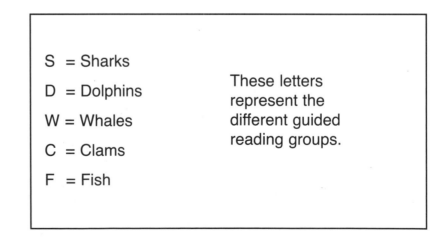

S = Sharks

D = Dolphins

W = Whales

C = Clams

F = Fish

These letters represent the different guided reading groups.

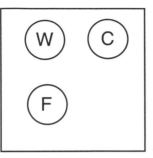

Squiggle

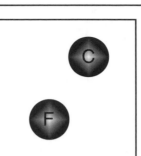

Wordless Books

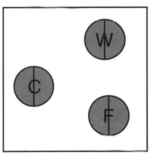

Cubes

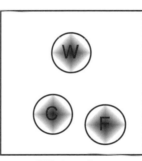

Flipbooks

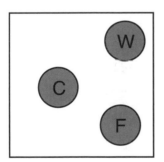

Listening Center

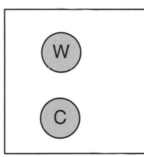

Character Picture

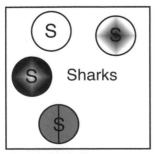

Sharks

Background Group

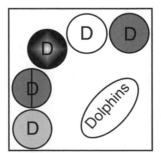

Dolphins

Guided Reading Groups

Quick Overview of Activities

Activity	Page	Changes made to the center after each two cycle rotation	First Grade Example	Second Grade Example	Third Grade Example
Top Ten	62	topic for the list of ten items	things that are red	favorite foods	mammals
Magazine Pictures Calendar Pictures Posters	65	new pictures and/or new skills to practice	write a sentence about each picture circle capital letters	choose a picture write a story	write sentences about each picture using contractions
Squiggle of the Week	67	new squiggle	write about the new squiggle picture	→	↑
Character Pictures	70	new character picture	put the character into a picture and write about it		↑
Letters and Notes	73	name of person to write to	write to a classmate	write a thank you letter	write a business letter
Journals	76	different topics	what I did at home last night	my pet	what I want to be when I grow up
Stackable Trays	76	different "fill-in" sheet	complete "fill-in"	→	
Wordless Books	76	different book	label pictures	write sentences about each page	write the text to the book
Authors	79	different topic	write a story		↑
Listening Station	81	different book and follow-up activities	draw the characters	write about the characters	compare and contrast you and a character

Activities (continued)

Activity	Page	Changes made to the center after each two cycle rotation	First Grade Example	Second Grade Example	Third Grade Example
Literary Friends	84	(this changes monthly) new literary friend	draw a picture and label	draw a picture and write at least three sentences	draw a picture and write a paragraph
Story Rewrites and Innovations	87	different book	writing based on book text	ay, a-e, ai, eigh	ay, a-e, ai, eigh
Flipbooks	89	topic for the flipbook	first, next, then, last	different types of weather	parts of speech (nouns, verbs, adjectives)
Find It In a Book	92	skills and examples to find	capital letters	quotation marks	verbs
Puppets and Headband Masks	93	different characters from a different book	Wild Things	Frog and Toad	Flat Stanley
Feltboards	94	different story	retell the story	⟶	retell the story and write summary
Storyboards	96	different book	make a story board	⟶	
Playing with Words	98	different pattern	ay	eigh	tion
Pull-Throughs and Flip-Overs	103	different pattern	at	ark	able
Walking the Room	104	skills and examples to find	letters of the alphabet	sight words	plurals

Activities (continued)

Activity	Page	Changes made to the center after each two cycle rotation	First Grade Example	Second Grade Example	Third Grade Example
Find It and Mark It Again and Again	105	different words	find the word(s)	→	→
Write a Sentence	106	different page in *Look-Alikes* or *Look-Alikes Jr.*	Look at the ____.	I found a ____ used as a ____.	use the dictionary to check spelling
Going, Going, Gone Clay or Playdough Sand or Salt Trays	107	different words	practice writing the words	→	→
Sentence Cubes	108	no change	roll, write, draw	→	use blank cubes to make sentence longer
Newspaper Detectives	111	skills and examples to find	"r" words	contractions	fact or opinion
Morning Message Station	112	(this changes daily) different message	work with different skills in the morning message	→	→
Mobiles	114	different topic or skill	colors	transportation	solid, liquid, gas

Part 4

Appendix

Book Lists

Organizing and Scheduling
Five Guided Reading Groups

Monday   Tuesday   Wednesday   Thursday   Friday

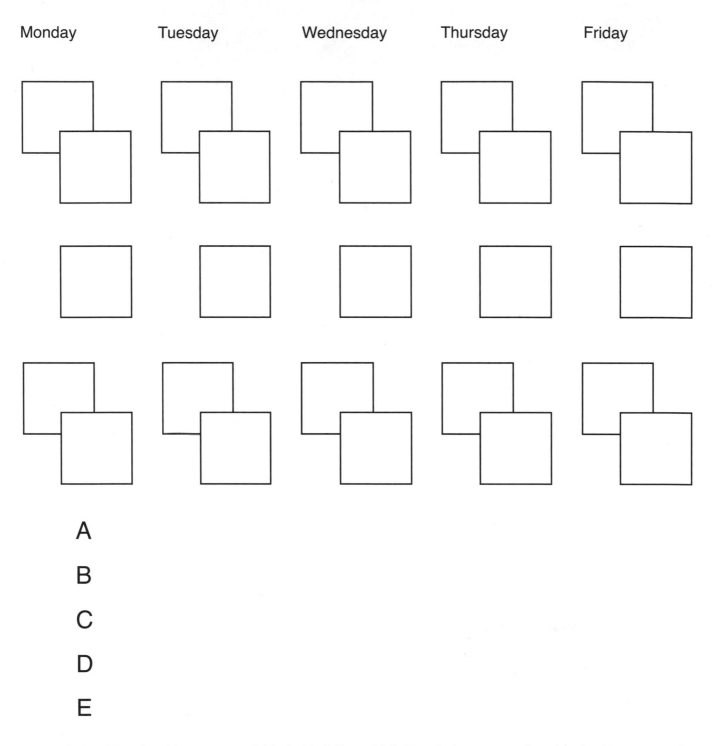

A

B

C

D

E

Organizing and Scheduling
Four Guided Reading Groups

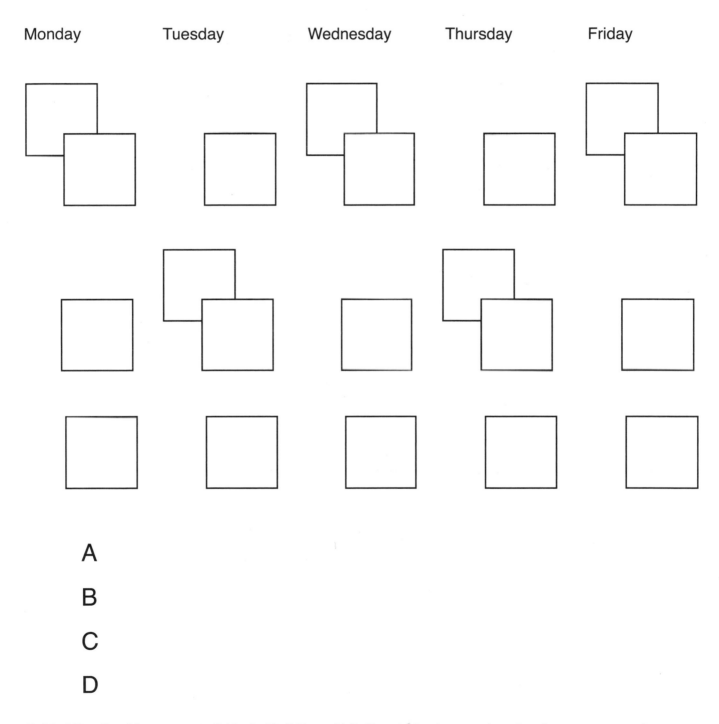

Monday	Tuesday	Wednesday	Thursday	Friday

A

B

C

D

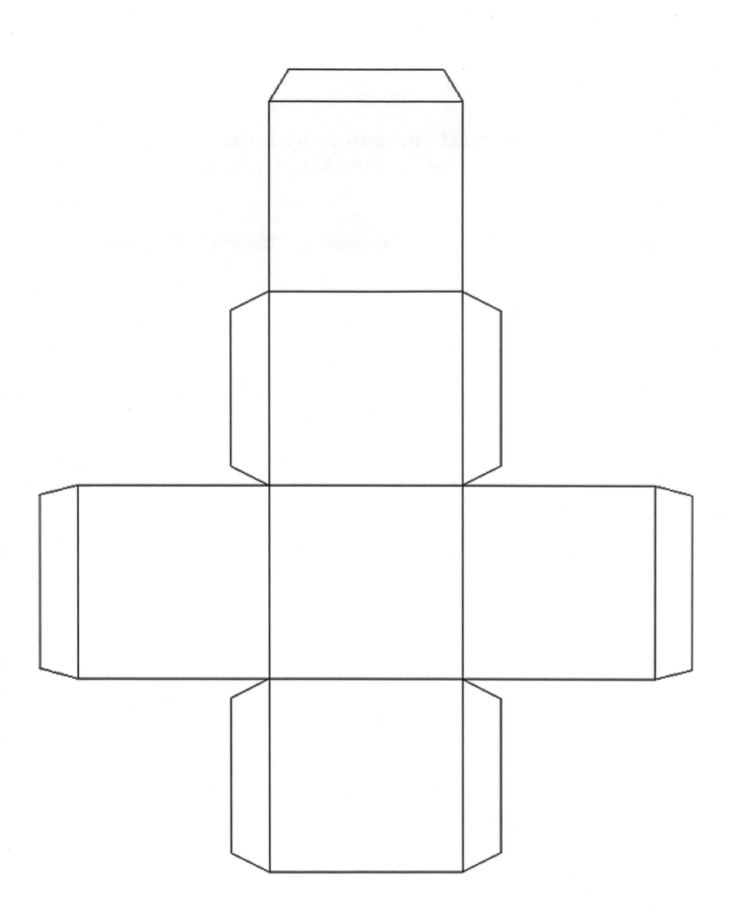

Name _____

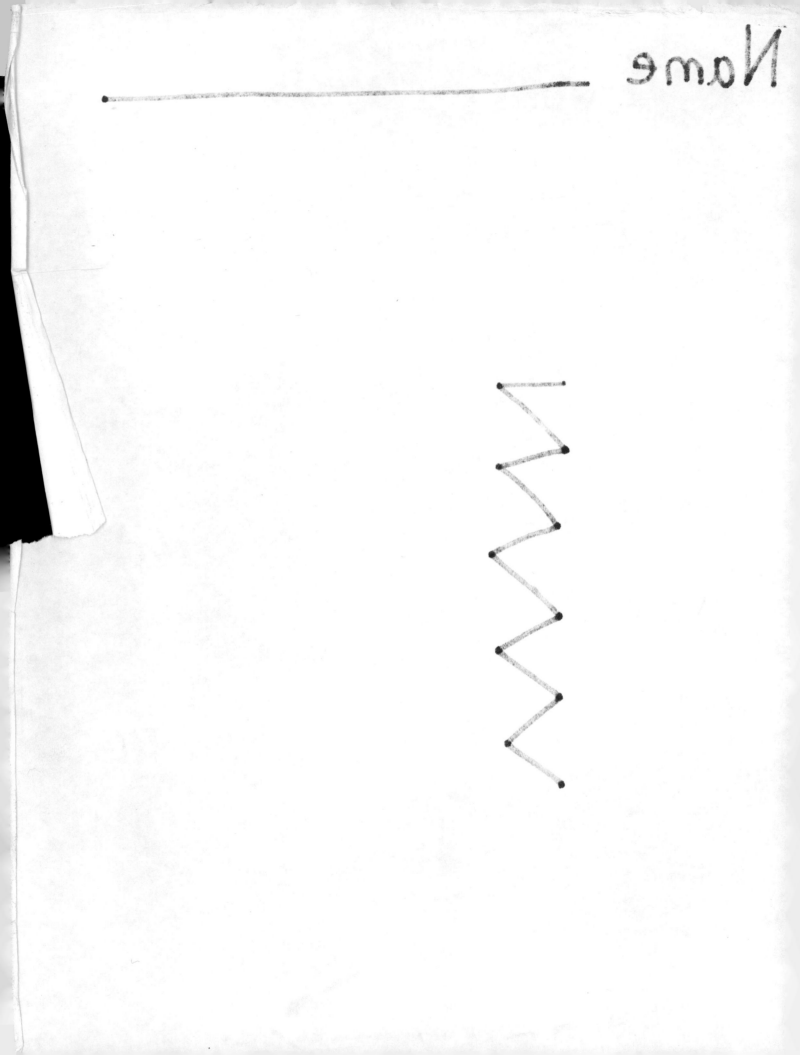

Name

Title of Article

Author

Fact	Opinion

Wordless Books

Title	Author
Alphabet City	Stephen Johnson
Changes Changes	Pat Hutchins
Deep in the Forest	Brinton Turkle
Dinosaur Day	Liza Donnelly
Eye Spy: A Book of Alphabet Puzzles	Linda Bourke
Flowers for the Snowman	Gerda Marie Scheidl
Free Fall	David Wiesner
Good Dog, Carl (series)	Alexandra Day
Oink	Arthur Geisert
Pancakes for Breakfast	Tomie DePaola
Picnic	Emily McCully
Rain	Peter Spier
Sector 7	David Wiesner
The Chicken's Child	Margaret Hartelius
The Grey Lady and the Strawberry Snatcher	Molly Bang
The Mysteries of Harris Burdick	Chris Van Allsburg
The Snowman	Raymond Briggs
Time Flies	Eric Rohmann
Tuesday	David Wiesner
We Hide, You Seek	Jose Aruego and Ariane Dewey
Why?	Nikolai Popov
You Can't Take a Balloon Into The Museum of Fine Arts	Jacqueline Preiss Weitzman and Robin Preiss Glasser
Zoom	Istvan Banya

Some of these books are available through Husky Trail Press LLC (huskytrailpress.com)

Eye Witness Readers
L 1-4

1-888-775-5211

152

Parts of Speech Books by Ruth Heller

Title	Skill
A Cache of Jewels	Collective Nouns
Behind the Mask	Prepositions
Fantastic! Wow! and Unreal!	Interjections and Conjunctions
Kites Sail High	Verbs
Many Luscious Lollipops	Adjectives
Merry-Go-Round	Nouns
Mine, All Mine	Pronouns
Up, Up and Away	Adverbs

Poetry Books

Title	Author
Big, Bad and a Little Bit Scary	Wade Zahares
Boston Tea Party	Pamela Duncan Edwards
A Burst of Firsts	J. Patrick Lewis
Casey At The Bat	Ernest Lawrence Thayer
I Invited a Dragon to Dinner	Chris L. Demarest
Laugh-eteria	Douglas Florian
Paul Revere's Ride	Henry Wadsworth Longfellow

The above books are available through Husky Trail Press LLC (huskytrailpress.com)

Point of View Books by Dr. Alvin Granowsky

These are two books in one. Read the original tale and then flip the book over for another point of view.

Title	Another Point of View
Cinderella	*That Awful Cinderella*
Goldilocks and the Three Bears	*Bears Should Share*
Henny Penny	*Brainy Bird Saves the Day*
Jack and the Beanstalk	*Giants Have Feelings Too*
Rumpelstiltskin	*A Deal Is a Deal*
Three Billy Goats Gruff	*Just a Friendly Old Troll*
Tortoise and the Hare	*Friends at the End*

Miscellaneous Books

Title	Author
Create Independent Learners (1-5)	Patricia Pavelka
The Jolly Postman	Janet & Alan Ahiberg
Look-Alikes	Joan Steiner
Look-Alikes Jr.	Joan Steiner
Making the Connection (K-2)	Patricia Pavelka
Making the Connection (3-6)	Patricia Pavelka

The above books are available through Husky Trail Press LLC (huskytrailpress.com)

Professional Reading and Resources

Allington, Richard L. & Patricia M. Cunningham. *Schools That Work: Where All Children Read and Write.* Boston, MA: Allyn and Bacon, 2002.

Byers, Gregg. *Teaching Guided Reading Strategies with Transparencies.* Greensboro, NC: Carson-Dellosa, 2001.

Campbell-Rush, Peggy. *I Teach Kindergarten: A Treasure Chest of Teaching Wisdom.* Peterborough, NH: Crystal Springs Books, 2000.

Campbell-Rush, Peggy. *Tricks of the Trade In & Out of the Classroom.* Peterborough, NH: Crystal Springs Books, 2001.

Cunningham, Patricia. *Guided Reading The Four-Blocks Way.* Greensboro, NC: Carson-Dellosa Publishing Company, Inc., 2000.

Cunningham, Patricia. *Making Words.* Torrance, CA: Good Apple, 1994.

Cunningham, Patricia. *Month-By-Month Phonics for 1st Grade.* Greensboro, NC: Carson-Dellosa Publishing Company, Inc., 1997.

Cunningham, Patricia. *Month-By-Month Phonics for 2nd Grade.* Greensboro, NC: Carson-Dellosa Publishing Company, Inc., 1998.

Cunningham, Patricia. *Teacher's Guide to the Four Blocks.* Greensboro, NC: Carson-Dellosa Publishing Company, Inc., 2000.

Feldman, Jean. *Transition Time: Let's do Something Different.* Beltsville, MD: Gryphon House, 1995.

Feldman, R. Jean. *Wonderful Rooms Where Children Can Bloom!* Peterborough, NH: Crystal Springs Books, 1997.

Fisher, Bobbi. *Thinking and Learning Together.* Portsmouth NH: Heinemann, 1995.

Fountas, Irene & Gay Su Pinnell. *Word Matters.* Portsmouth, NH: Heinemann, 1998.

Fountas, Irene & Gay Su Pinnell. *Guided Reading.* Portsmouth, NH: Heinemann, 2000.

Fountas, Irene & Gay Su Pinnell. *Guiding Readers and Writers.* Portsmouth, NH: Heinemann, 2001.

Fountas, Irene & Gay Su Pinnell. *Matching Books to Readers.* Portsmouth, NH: Heinemann, 1999.

Gravois, Michael. *35 Ready-To-Go Ways to Publish Students' Research and Writing: Grades 4-8.* New York, NY: Scholastic Professional Books, 1998.

Hall, Dorothy P. and Elaine Williams. *The Teacher's Guide to Building Blocks.* Greensboro, NC: Carson-Dellosa, 2000.

Hart-Hewins, Linda. *Better Books! Better Readers!* York, ME: Stenhouse Publishers, 1999.

Hill, Susan. *Guiding Literacy Learners.* York, ME: Stenhouse Publishers, 1999.

Holliman, Linda. *Teachin' Cheap: Using Bags, Sacks, Paper, & Boxes in the Classroom.* Cypress, CA: Creative Teaching Press, Inc., 1997.

Ingraham, Phoebe Bell. *Creating & Managing Learning Centers: A Thematic Approach.* Peterborough, NH: Crystal Springs Books, 1997.

MacDonald, Sharon. *Idea Bags: Activities to Promote the School-to-Home Connection.* Torrance, CA: Fearon Teacher Aids, 1999.

MacDonald, Sharon. *Squish, Sort, Paint & Build: Easy Learning Center Activities.* Beltsville, MD: Gryphon House, 1996.

McCarrier, Andrea and Gay Su Pinnell. *Interactive Writing: How Language and Literacy Come Together* (K-2). Portsmouth, NH: Heinemann, 2000.

Nations, Susan & Mellissa Alonso. *Primary Literacy Centers: Making Reading and Writing Stick.* Gainesville, FL: Maupin House Publishing, Inc., 2001.

Pavelka, Patricia. *Create Independent Learners* (1-5). Peterborough, NH: Crystal Springs Books, 1999.

Pavelka, Patricia. *Making the Connection: Learning Skills Through Literature* (K-2). Peterborough, NH: Crystal Springs Books, 1995.

Pavelka, Patricia. *Making the Connection: Learning Skills Through Literature* (3-6). Peterborough, NH: Crystal Springs Books, 1997.

Pilgreen, L. Janice. *The SSR Handbook: How to Organize and Manage a Sustained Silent Reading Program.* Portsmouth, NH: Boynton/Cook Publishers, Inc., 2000.

Schulman, Browning. *Guided Reading: Making it Work.* New York, NY: Scholastic Professional Books, 2000.

Sigmon, Cherly Mahaffey. *Implementing the 4-Blocks Literacy Model.* Greensboro, NC: Carson-Dellosa Publishing Company, Inc., 1997.

Szymusiak, Karen. *Beyond Leveled Books.* Portland, ME: Stenhouse Publishers, 2001.

Taberski, Sharon. *On Solid Ground.* Portsmouth, NH: Heinemann, 2000.

Thompson, A. Ellen. *I Teach First Grade!* Peterborough, NH: Crystal Springs Books, 2001.

Trelease, Jim. *The New Read-Aloud Handbook.* New York, NY: Penguin Group, 2001.

Weaver, M. Brenda. *Leveling Books K-6.* Newark, DE: International Reading Association, 2000.

Zgonc, Yvette. *Sounds in Action. Phonological Awareness.* Peterborough, NH: Crystal Springs Books, 2000.

Many of these books are available through Crystal Springs Books, 10 Sharon Road, PO Box 500, Peterborough, NH 03458, 1-800-321-0401

Bring the author to your school

Patricia Pavelka's dynamic workshops for Teachers and Administrators of grades K-8 include:

- ❏ Guided Reading Instruction and Management
- ❏ Content Area Reading and Study Strategies
- ❏ Effective Reading Strategies for Struggling Students
- ❏ Flexible Grouping
- ❏ Learning Centers
- ❏ Writing Workshop
- ❏ Managing a Wide Range of Learners

Inspiring keynote presentations by Pat are also available

The illustrator, Deborah Gillette-Youngblood, is a Special Education Teacher with a Master of Science Degree in Learning Disabilities. Debbie has worked with visual arts (drawing, painting and photography) since she was a child.

Debbie enjoys gardening and other outdoor activities and raising her two children in Connecticut.

This book's mascot is Beaker, a very loud Amazon Parrot who is 30 years old.

Husky Trail Press LLC is based on the courage, leadership, and loyalty of the Husky. The Husky's ability to always do its very best and excel, no matter how difficult the obstacles, is an encouragement to us all.